I KNOW MY RIGHTS!

A Colorful World of Children's Rights

Coloring Book by Anna Gilchrist

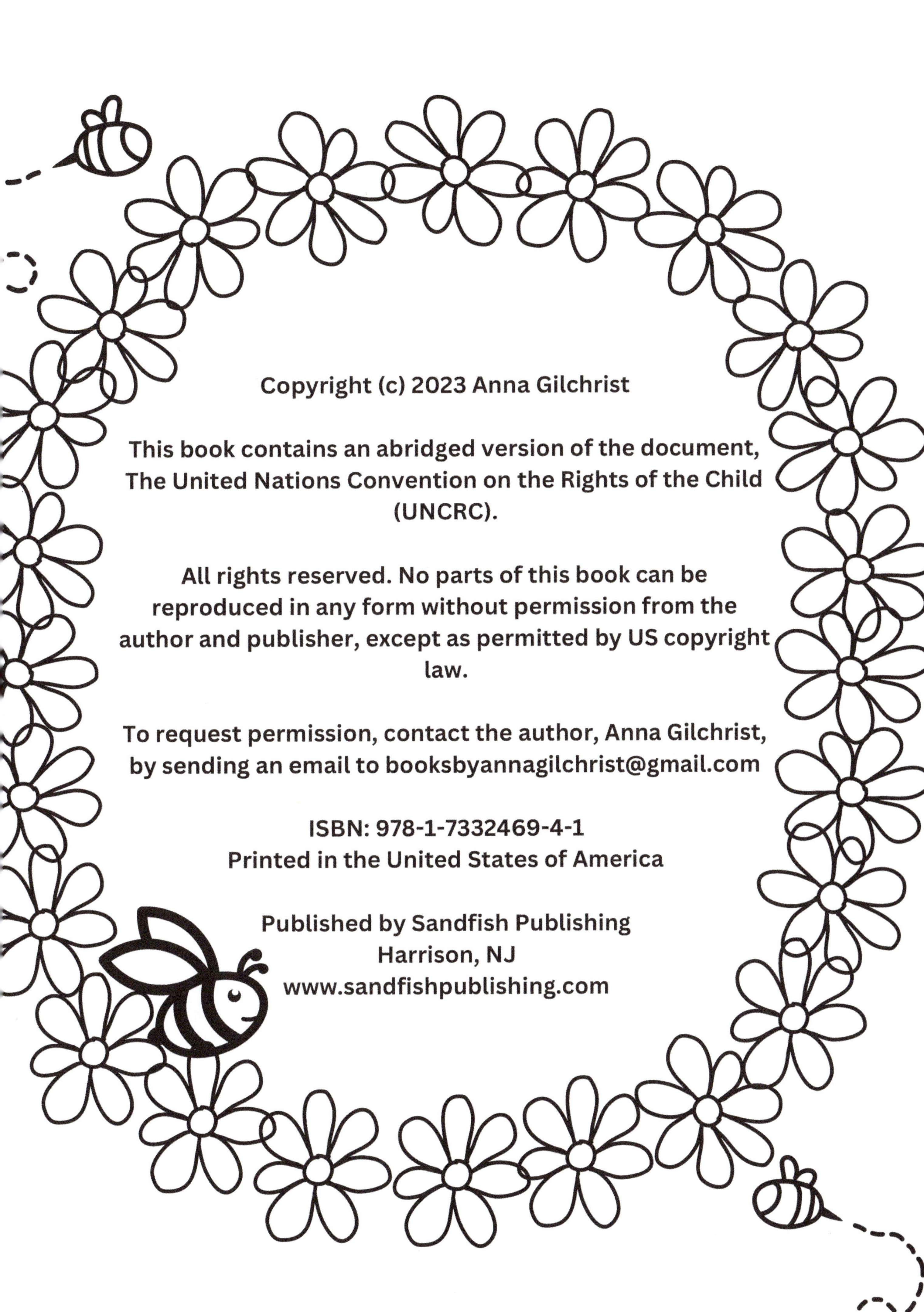

ISBN: 978-1-7332469-4-1
Printed in the United States of America

Published by Sandfish Publishing
Harrison, NJ
www.sandfishpublishing.com

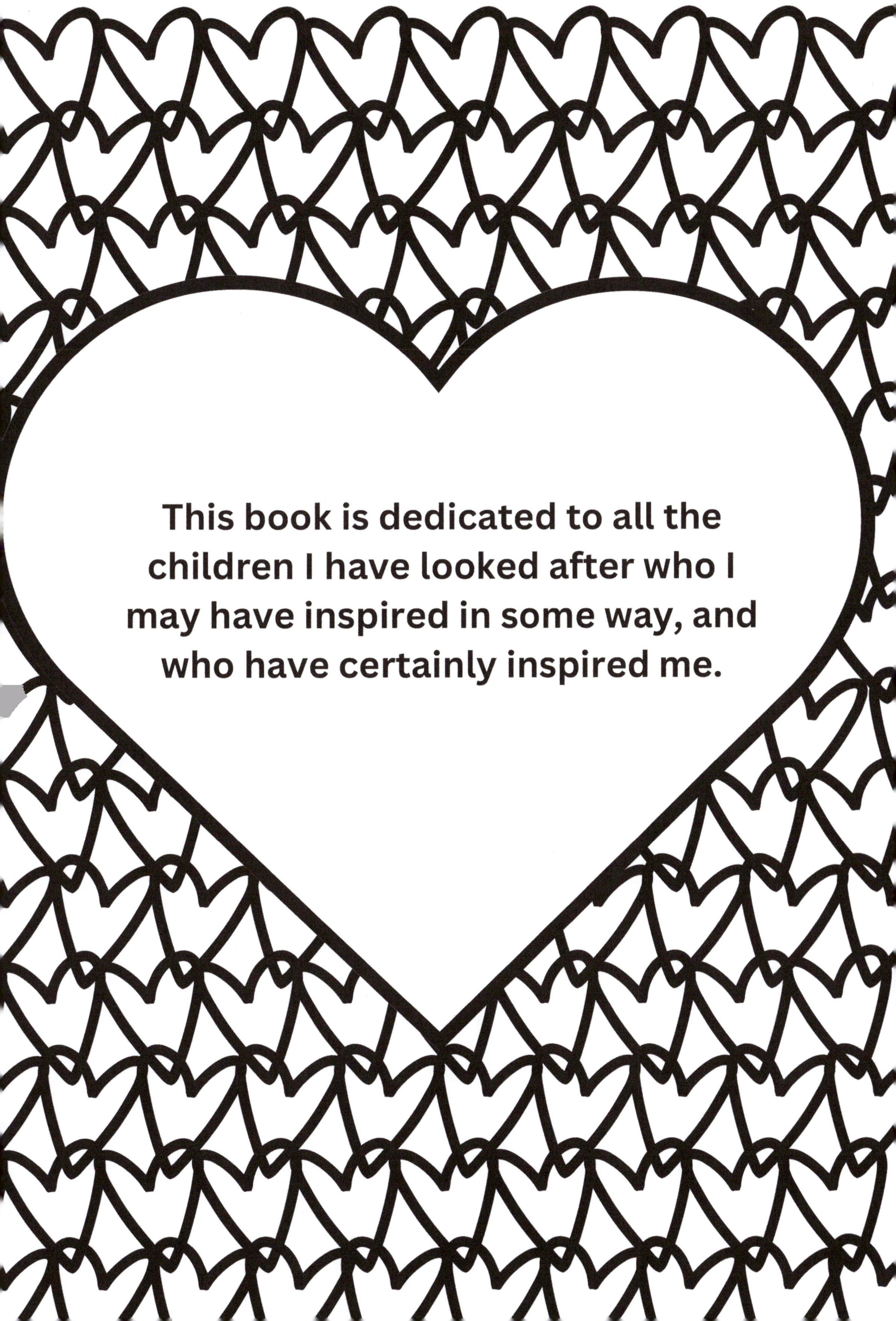
This book is dedicated to all the children I have looked after who I may have inspired in some way, and who have certainly inspired me.

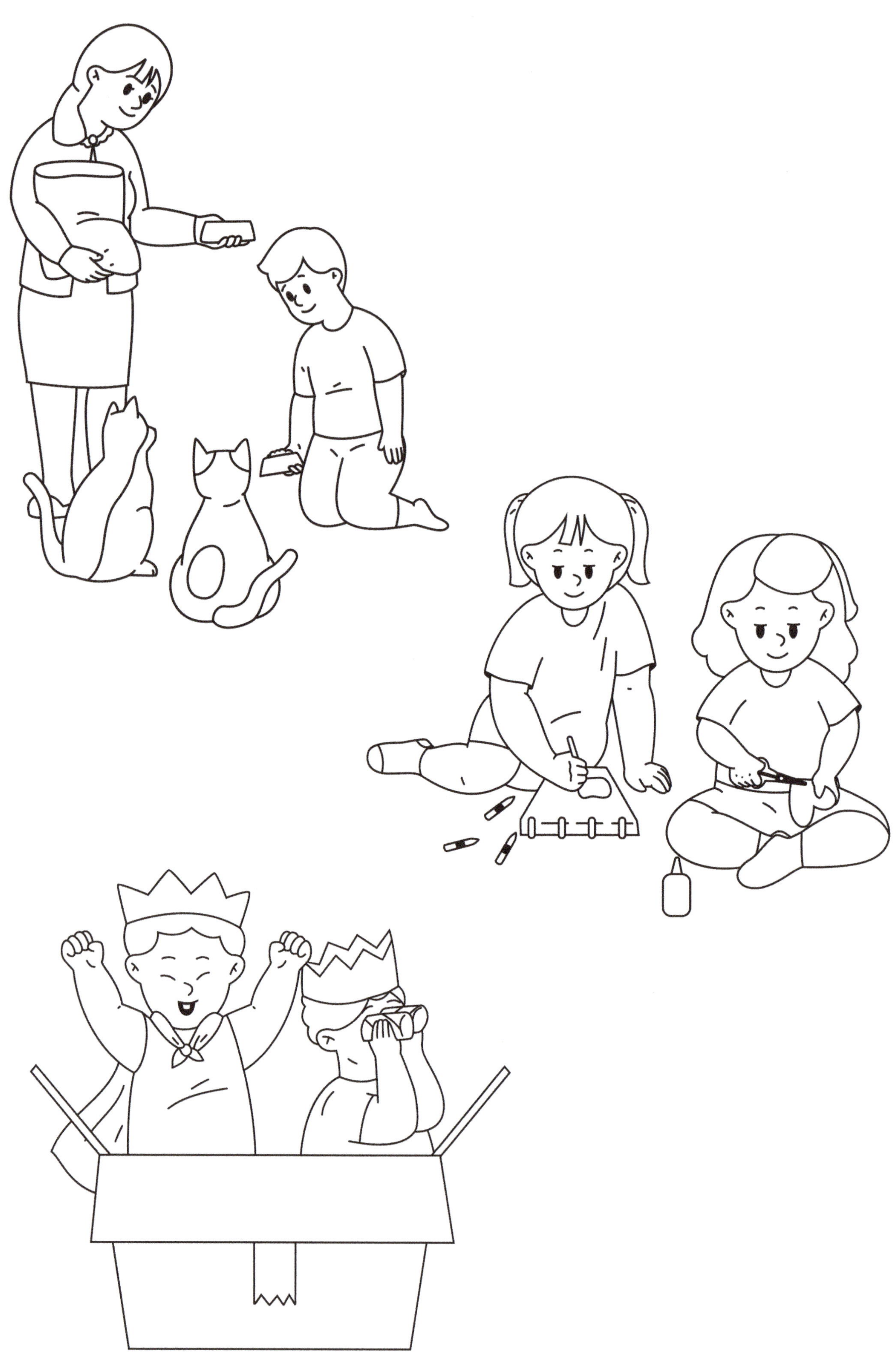

I KNOW MY RIGHTS!

First of all... What are Children's Rights?

Children's rights are the unique human rights children have and are entitled to. They are specialized for young people since they are a special group in need of guidance, protection, and safeguarding.

Why are they important?

It is important for all people - including children - to know their rights so they will know when they are being mistreated or taken advantage of. That way, a person can speak up and make sure they receive the respect they deserve.

Where can I read more about them?

A list of all children's rights is available in a document called the United Nations Convention on the Rights of the Child (UNCRC). It can be found online, but since it is for adults to read, it can be long and wordy.

Fortunately, all the children's rights in this coloring book are listed in a way that is easier to understand so you can learn and know your rights!

Ask a grown-up to help you if you have questions about any of the rights you see in this book.

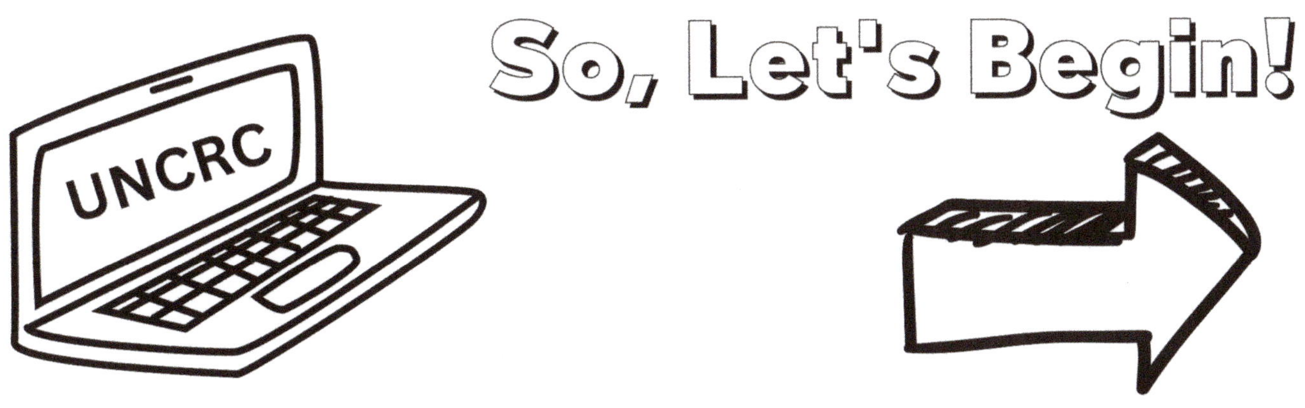

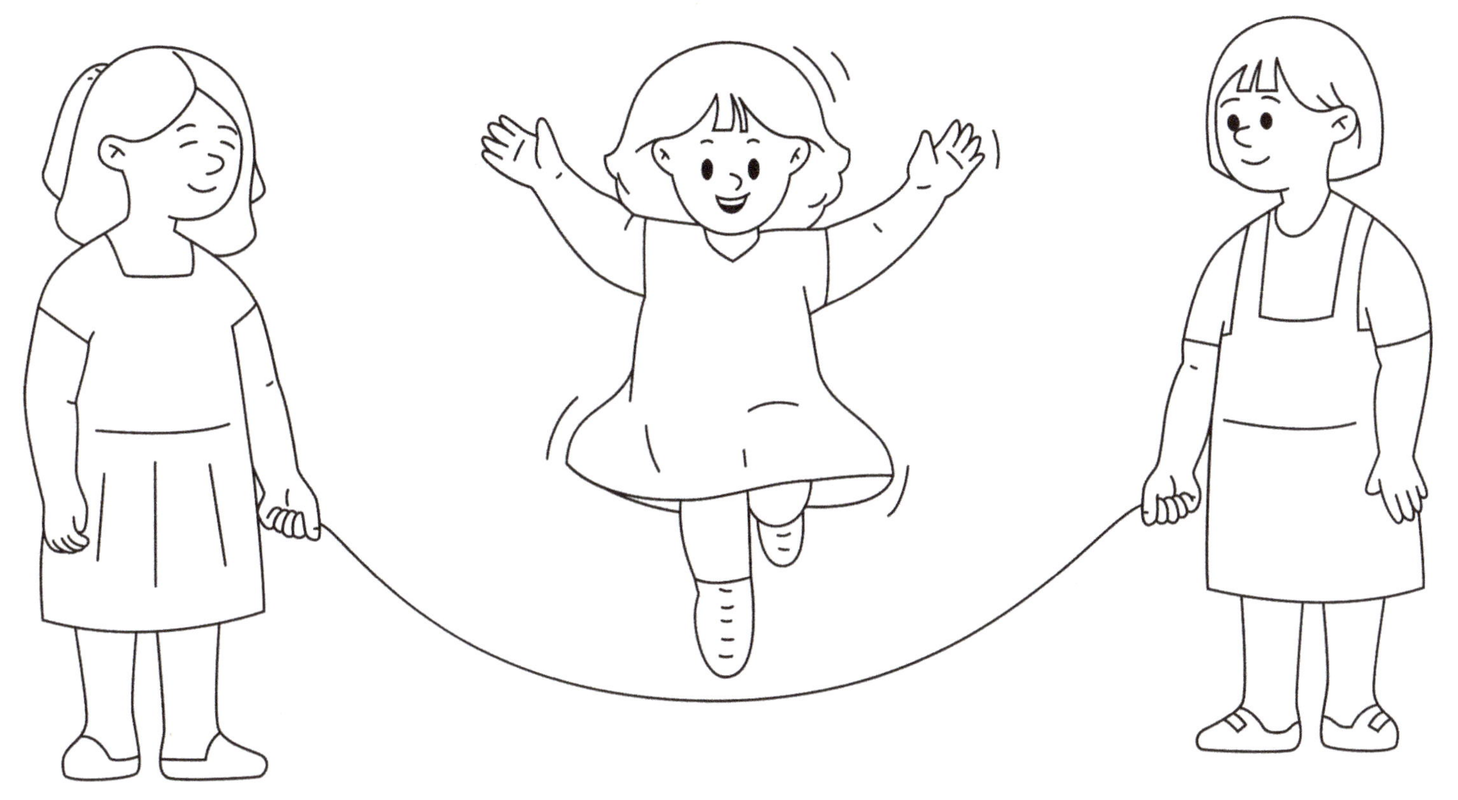

1.
Every child or person under the age of 18 has human rights.

2.

Every child has rights, regardless of ethnicity, gender, religion, language, abilities, or cultural background.

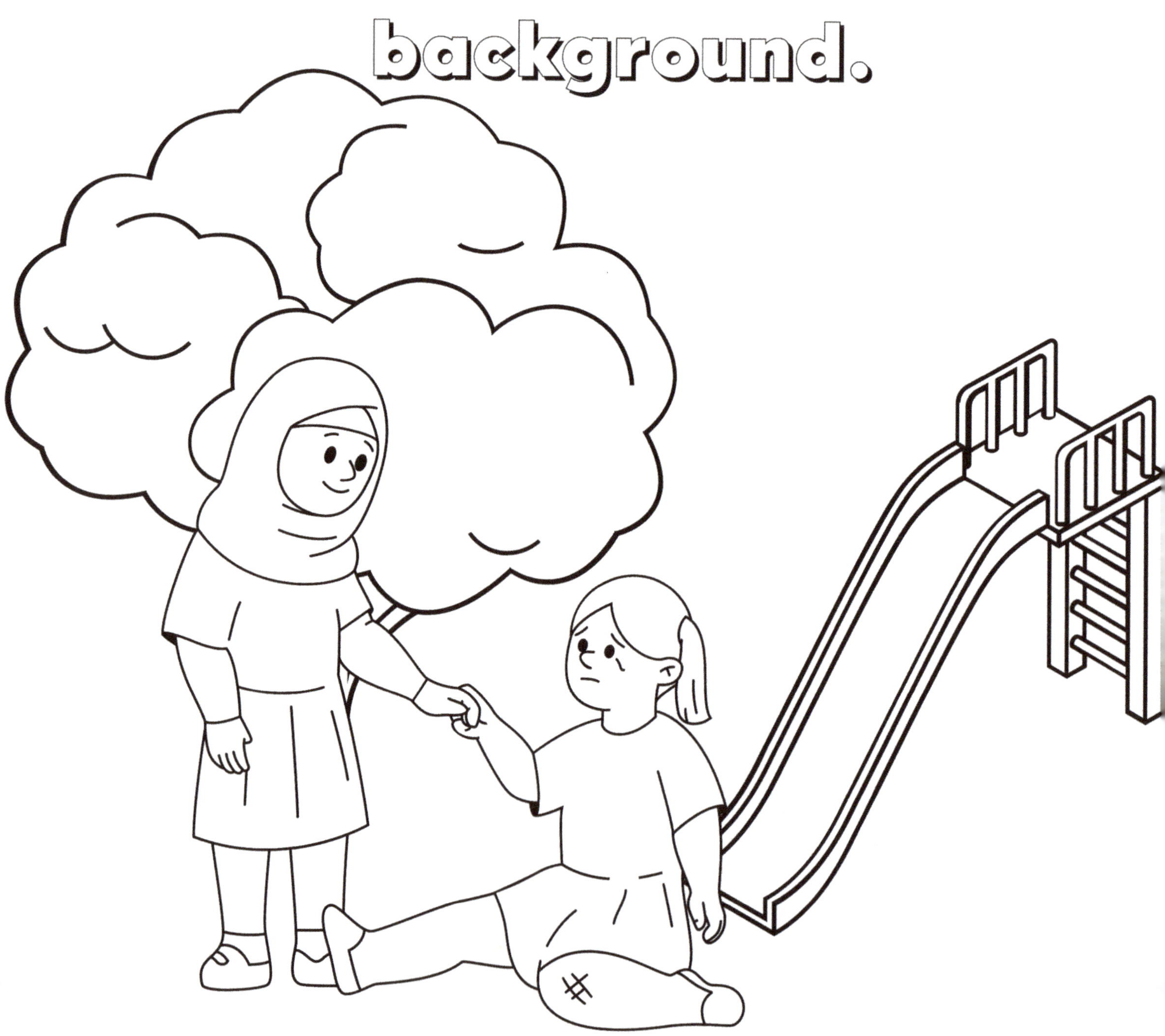

3.
Any decision made for any child should always be in the child's best interest.

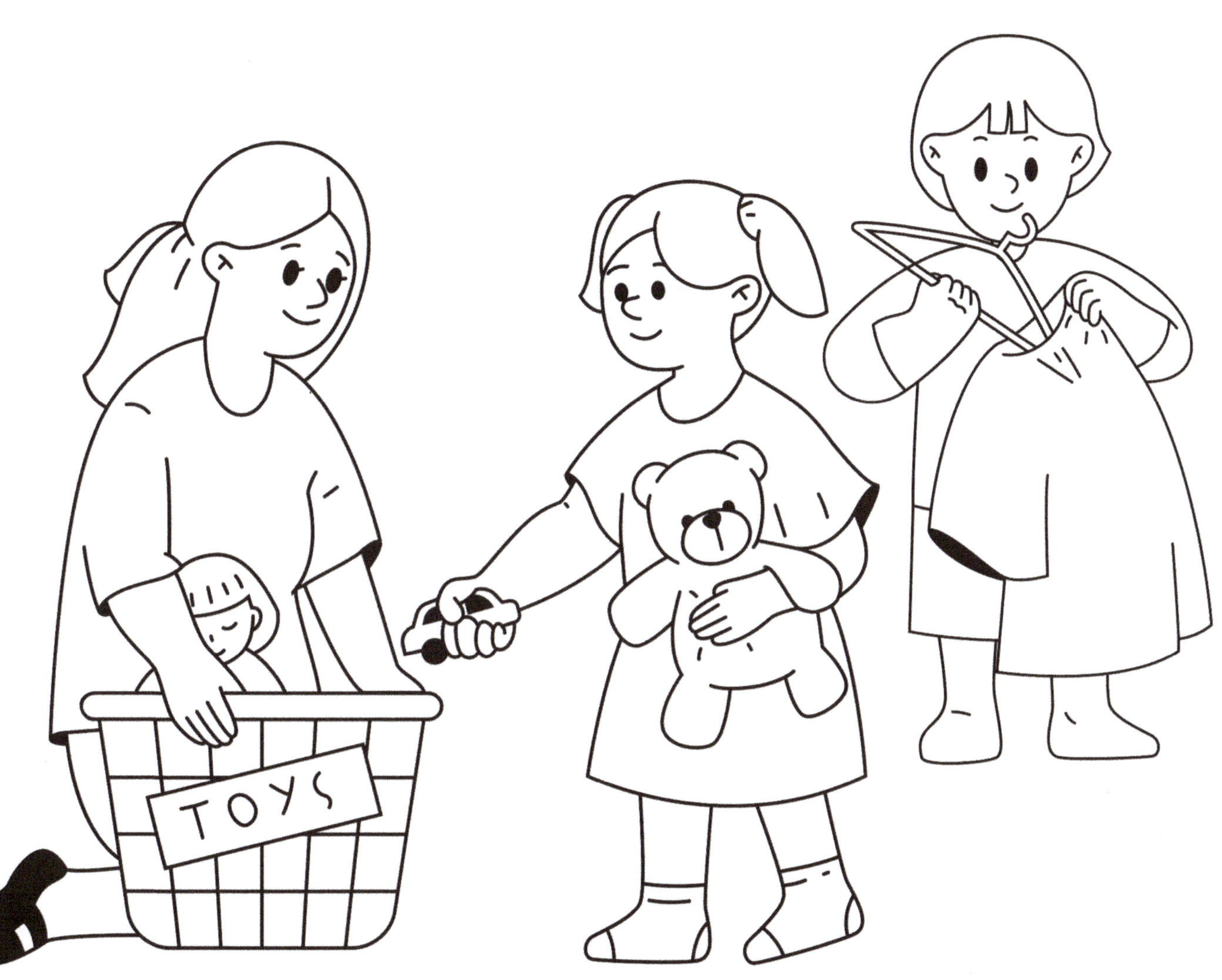

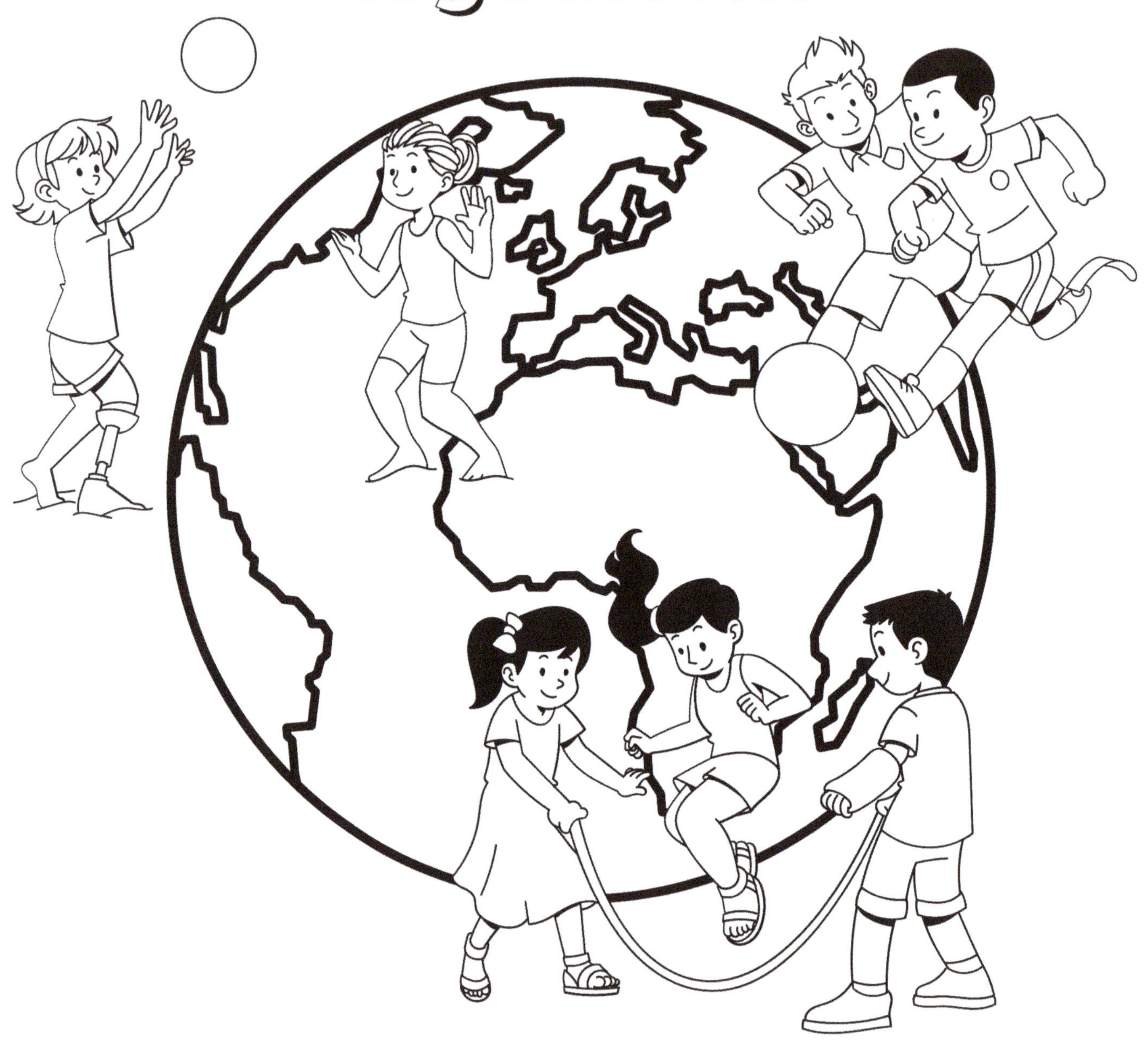

4.
The world should work together...

...to protect the rights of every child.

5.

Every child deserves parents or guardians who provide them with proper guidance and support.

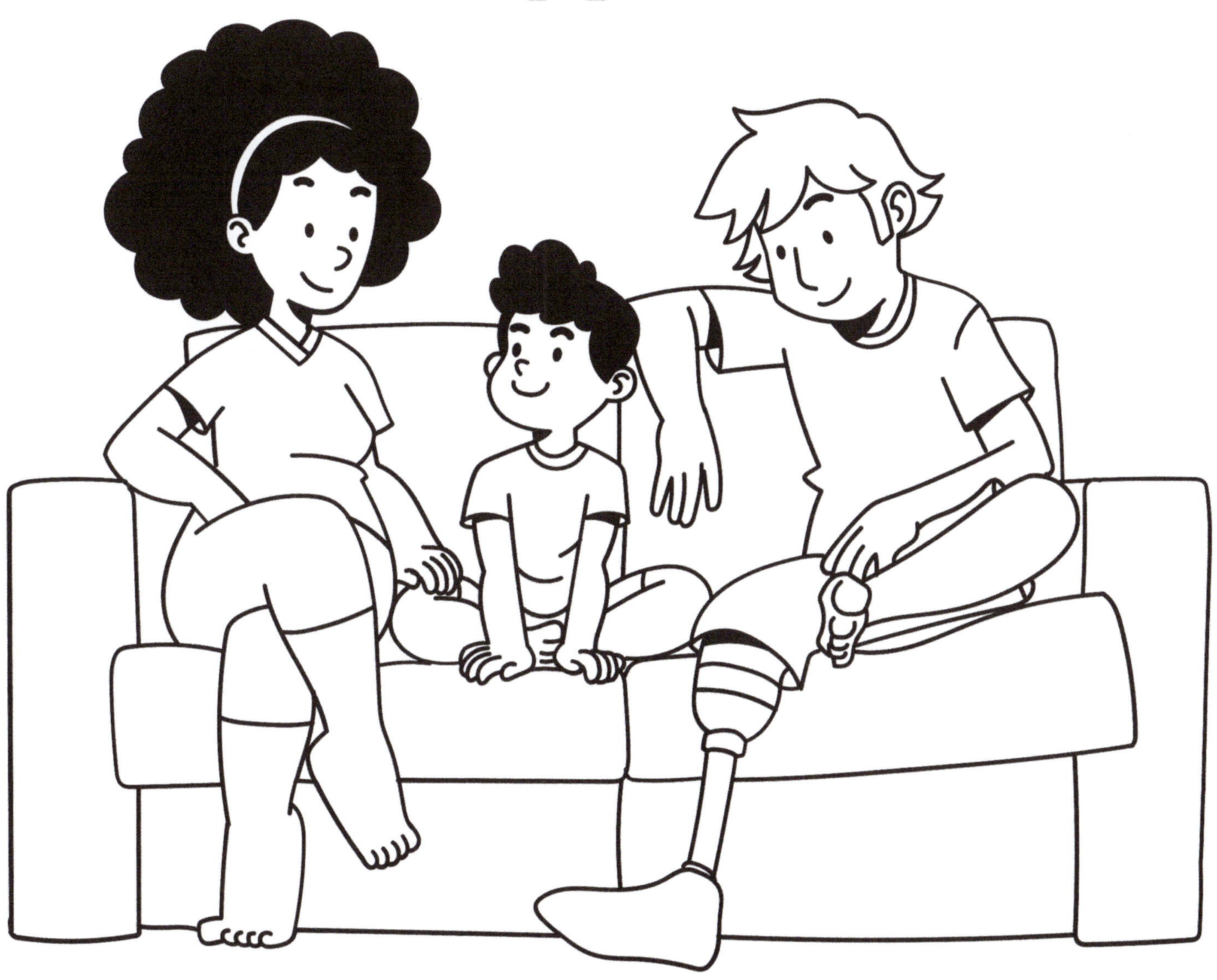

6.

Every child has the right to live, survive, and grow to their full potential.

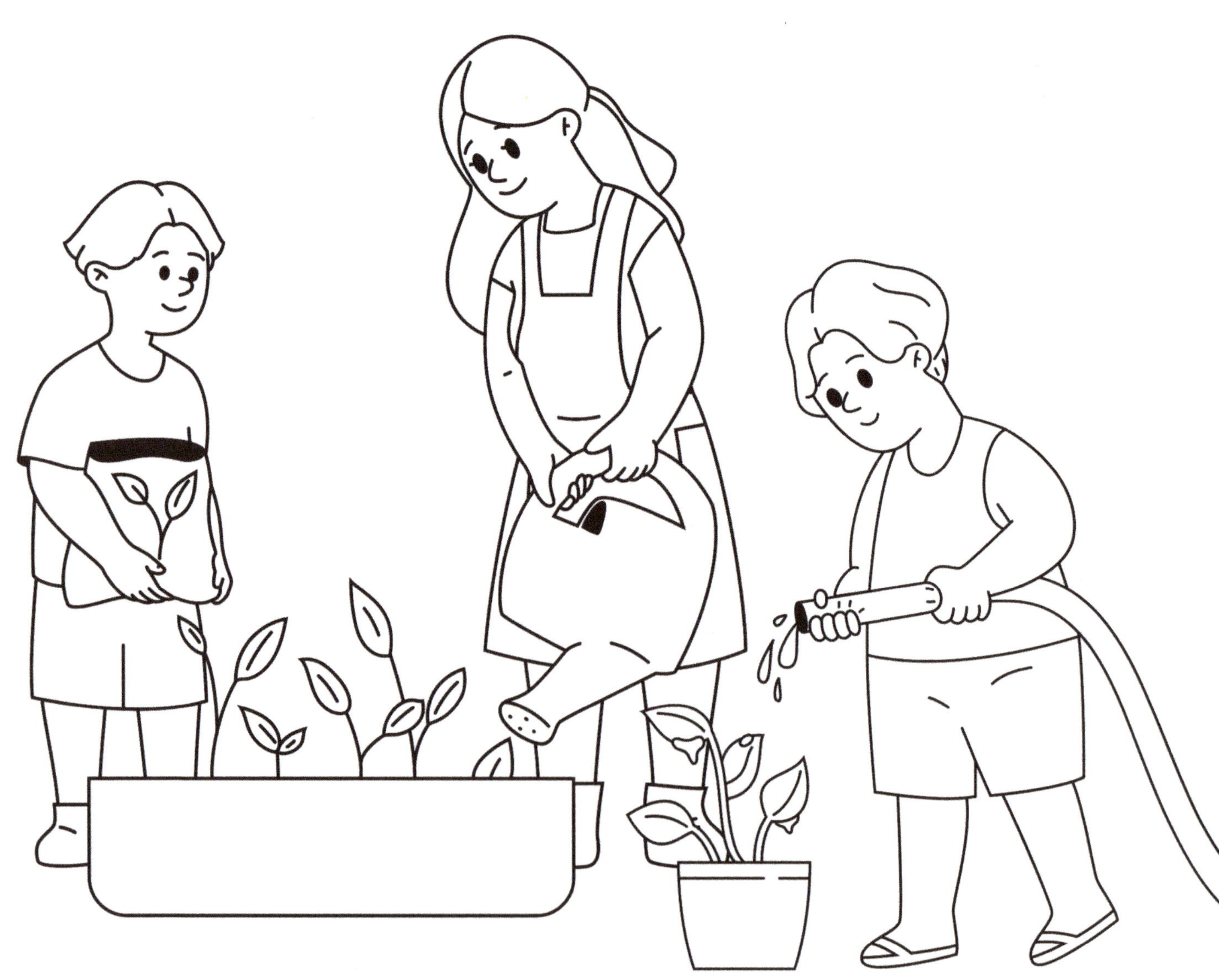

7.

Every child should have a name and nationality that is recorded and officially recognized at birth. They should also be loved and cared for by their parents or guardian.

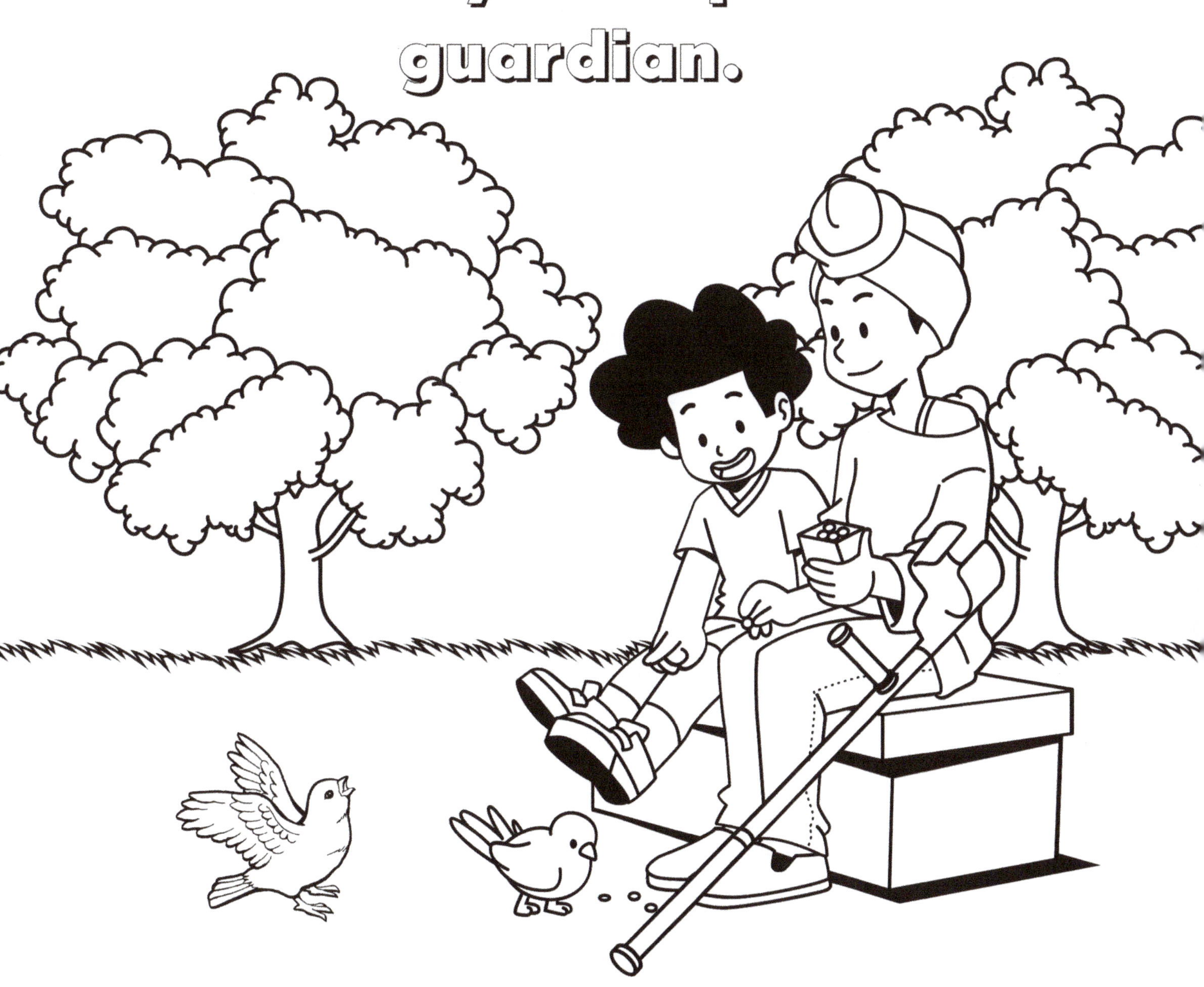

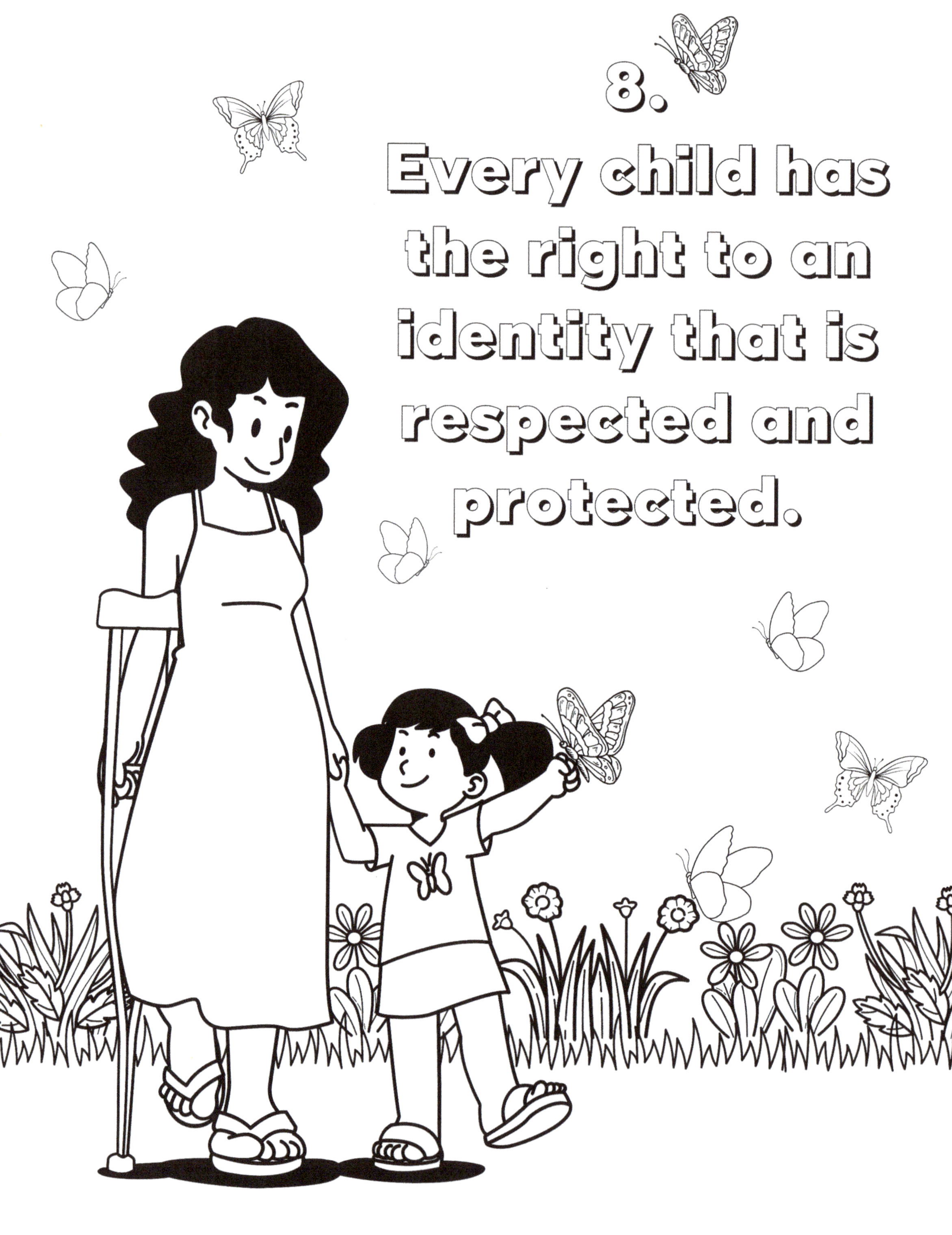

8.
Every child has the right to an identity that is respected and protected.

9.

Every child has the right to be with and be in contact with their parents or guardian...

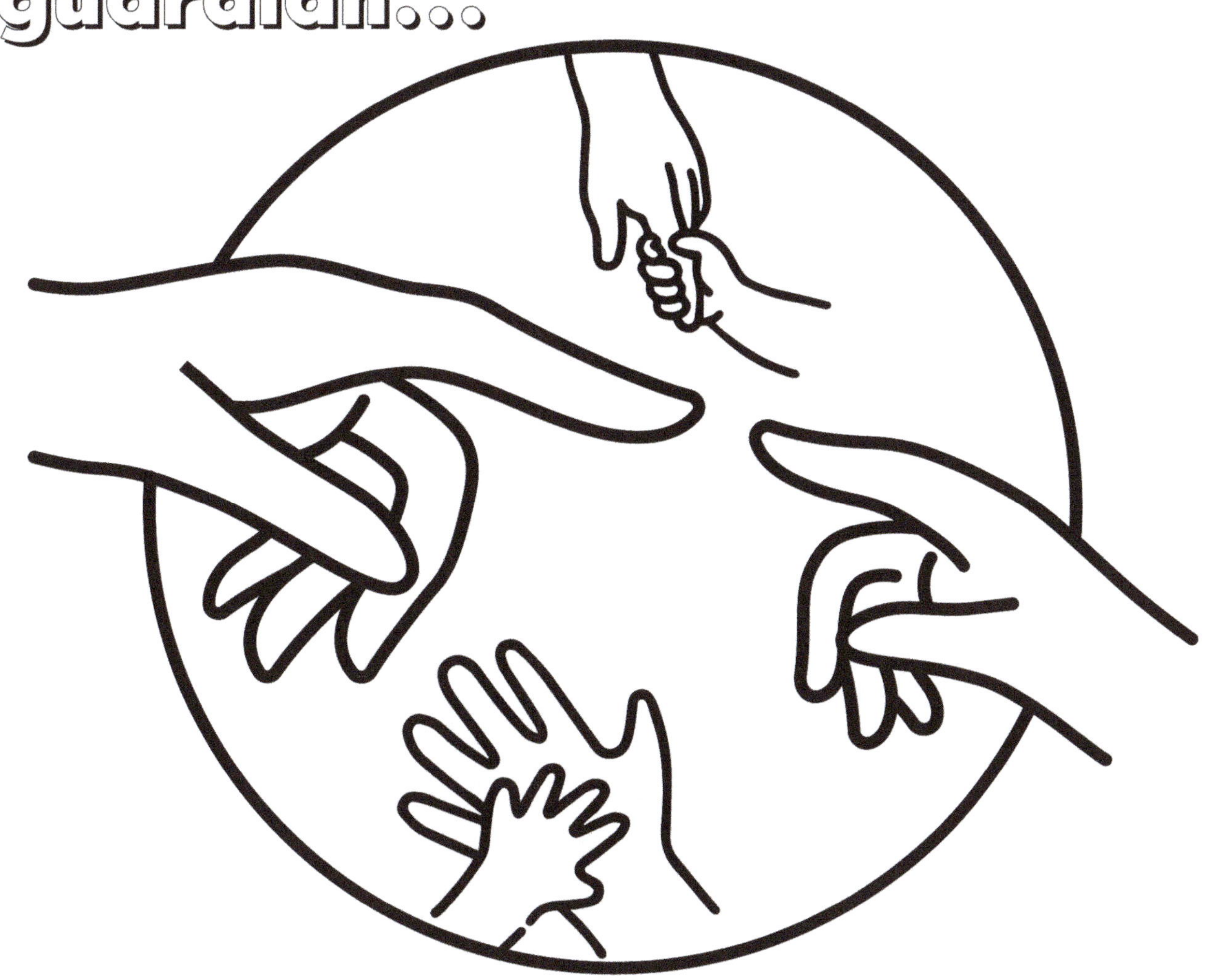

...and they should not be separated from them against their will except in the case of child abuse and neglect.

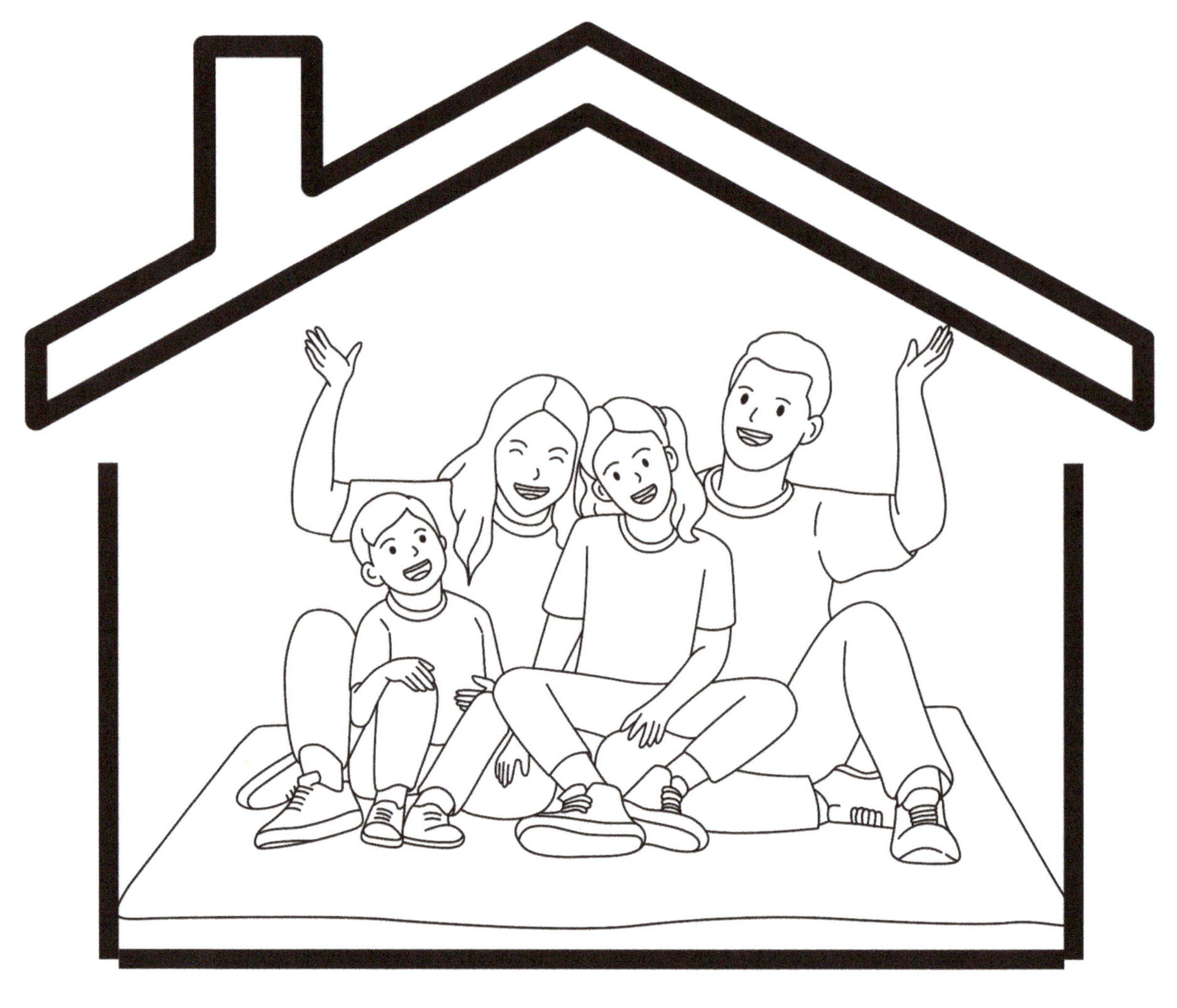

10.

Every child should be able to live with their parents in the same country and stay in contact with their parents who may live in a different country from them.

11.
Every child should be protected from being kidnapped or removed from their own country illegally by their parents or other family members.

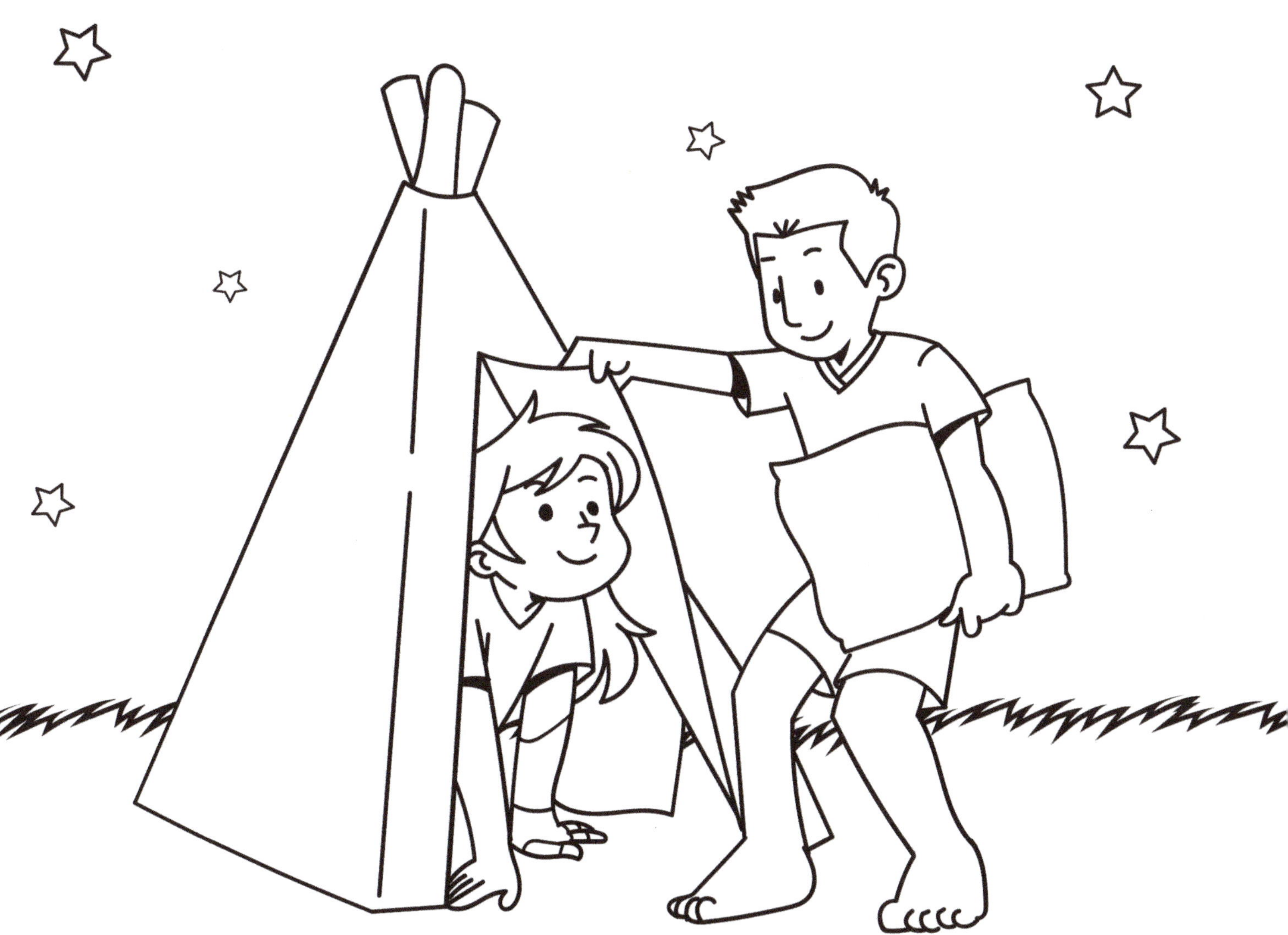

12.
Every child has the right to express their thoughts, feelings, and ideas regarding their personal matters, and to be taken seriously about the issues affecting them at all times.

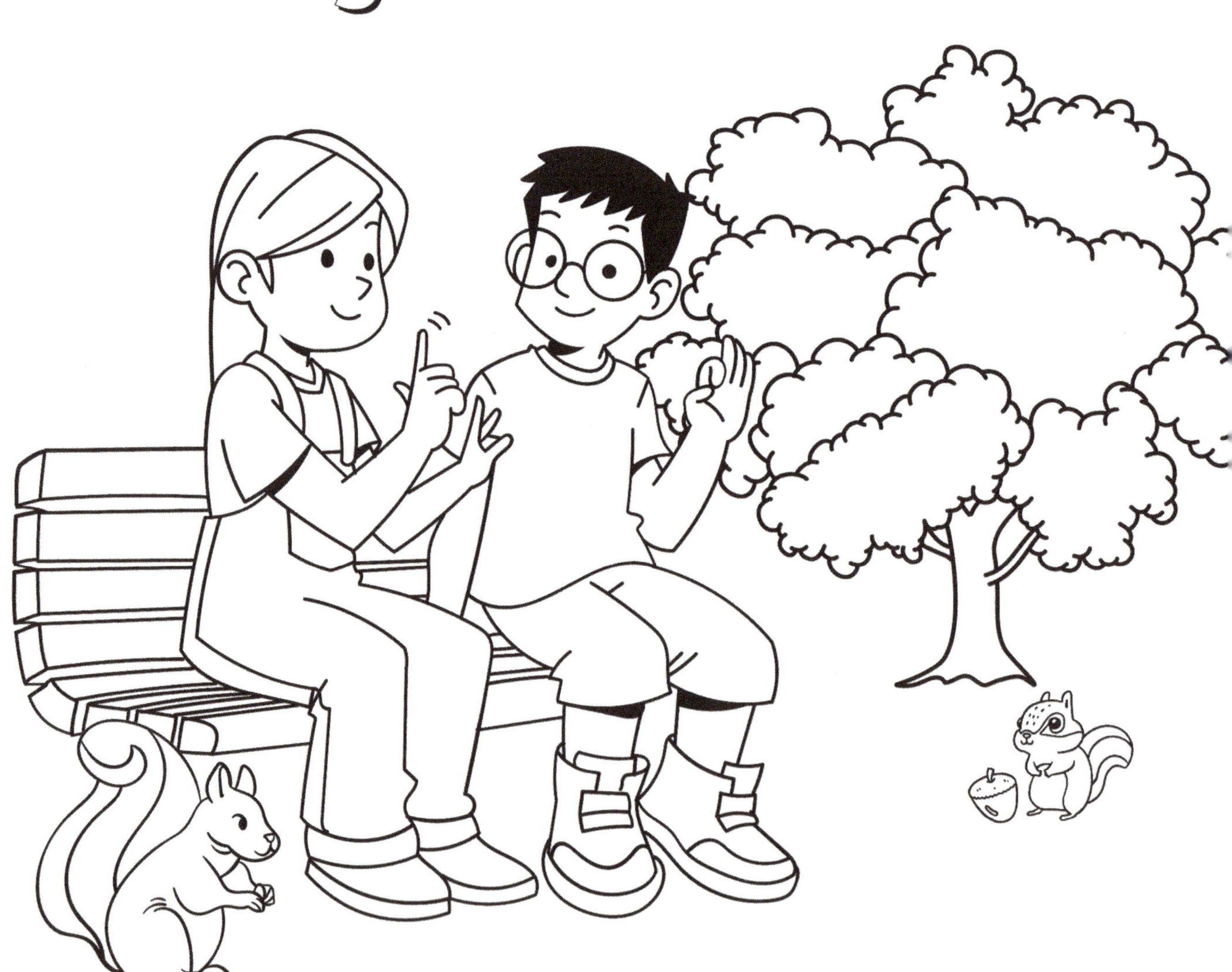

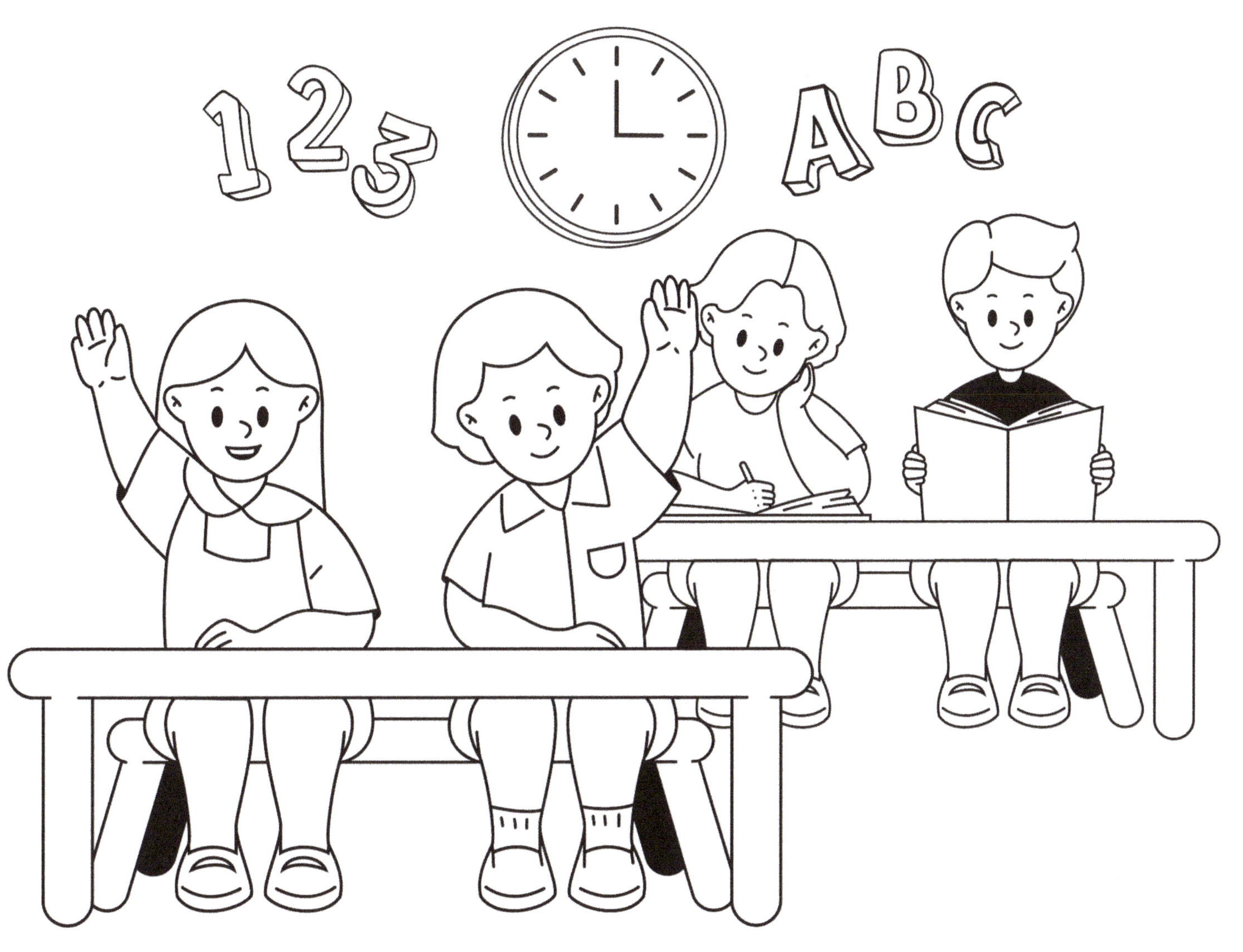

13.

Every child has the right to express their thoughts and opinions, and have an education so they may continue to expand their knowledge about the world.

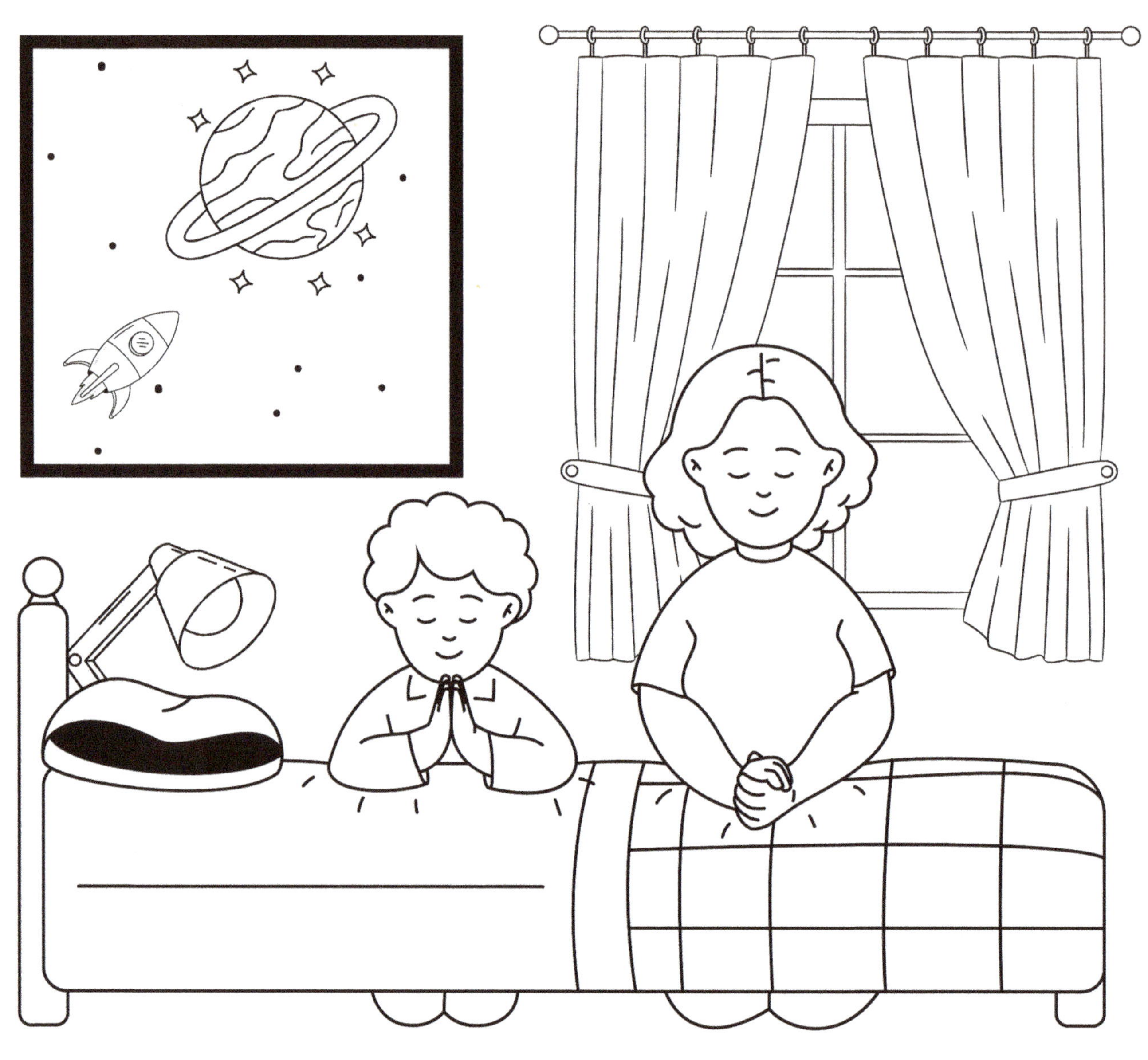

14.

Every child has a right to believe or practice any faith or religion they choose, while also learning to respect the different beliefs and faiths of others.

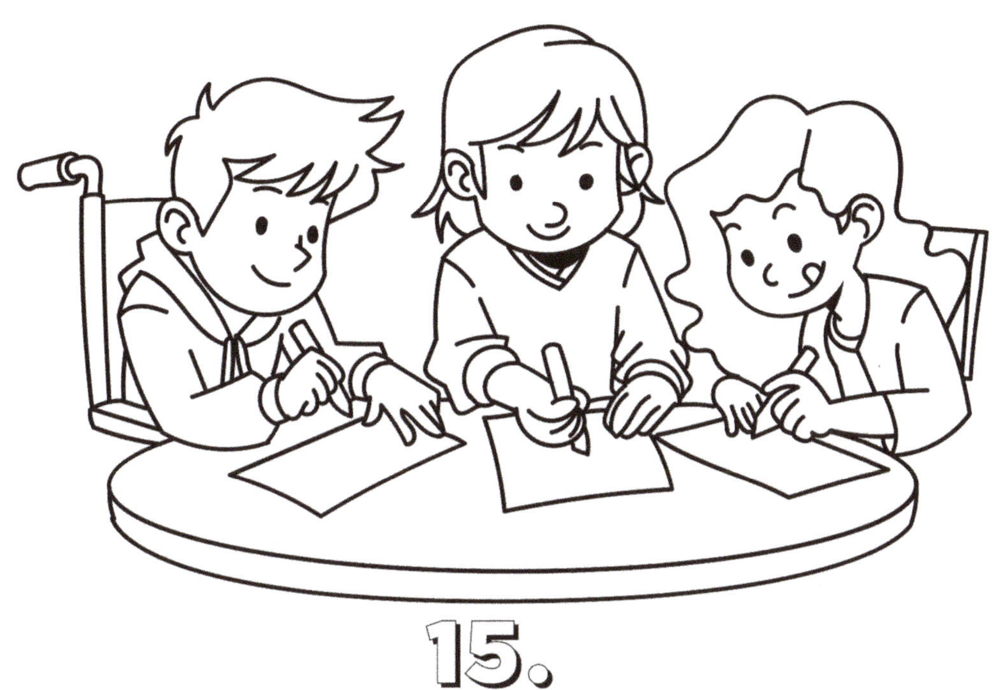

15.

Every child has the right to meet with and participate in groups and organizations with other children.

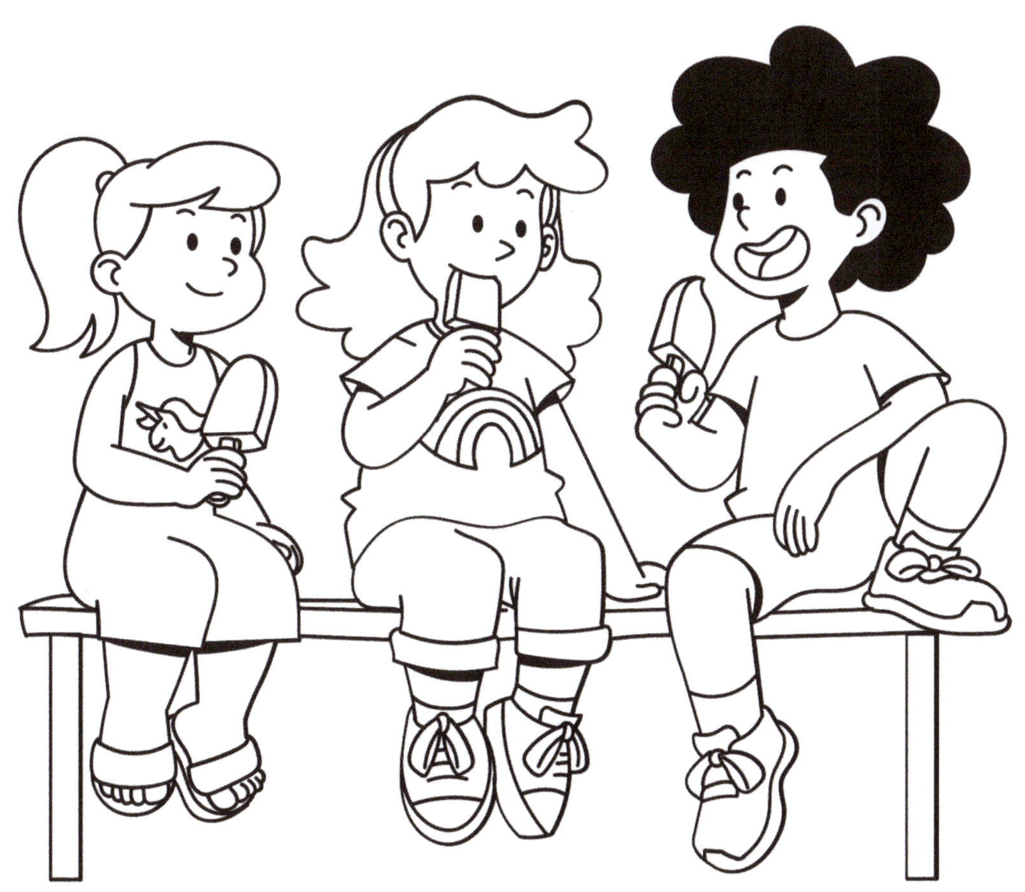

16.
Every child has the right to privacy with a private family, school, and home life, and to have their privacy protected.

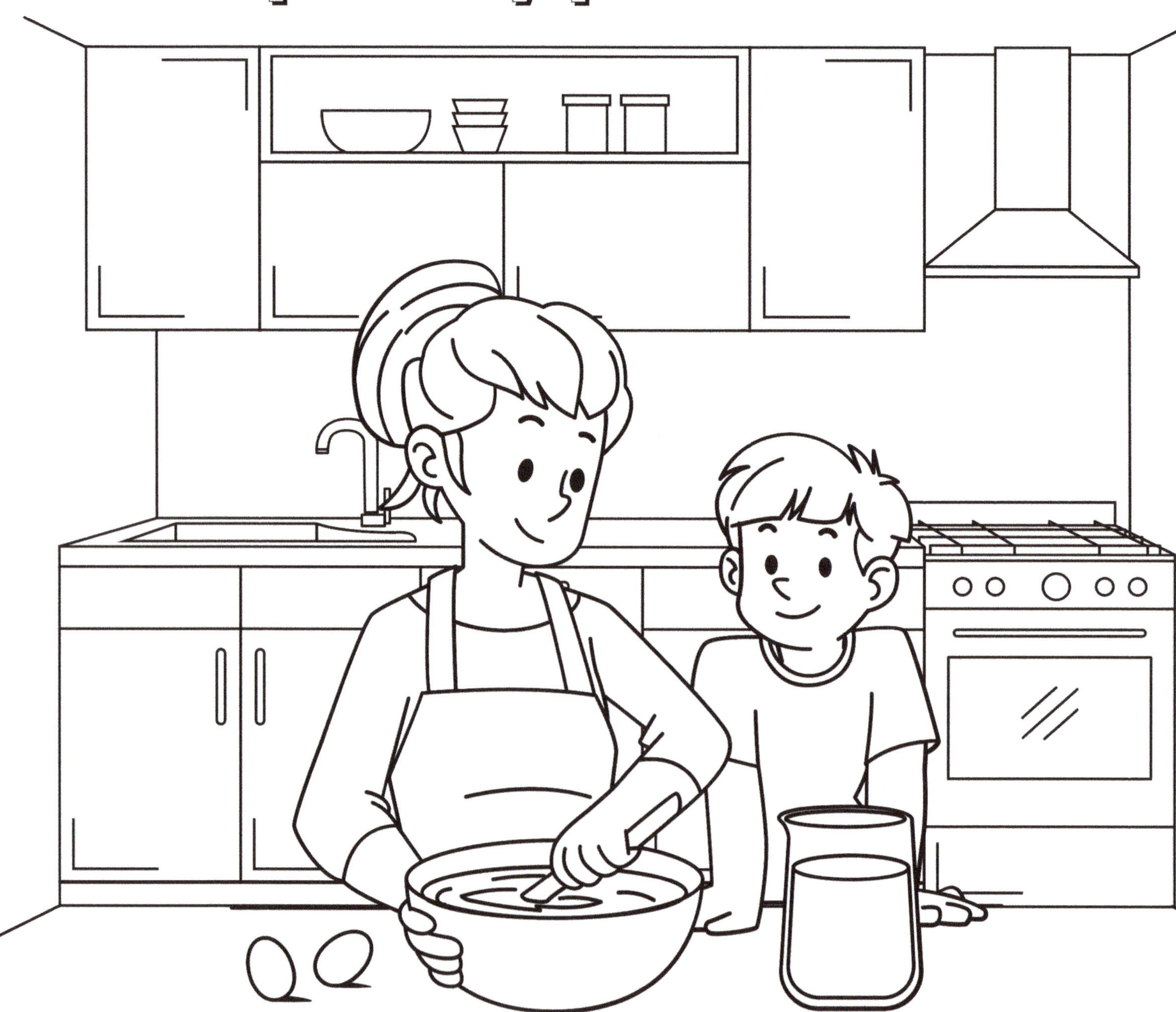

17.

Every child has the right to obtain information from media sources - like the Internet, TV, and movies - and to be protected from media sources that may cause them harm.

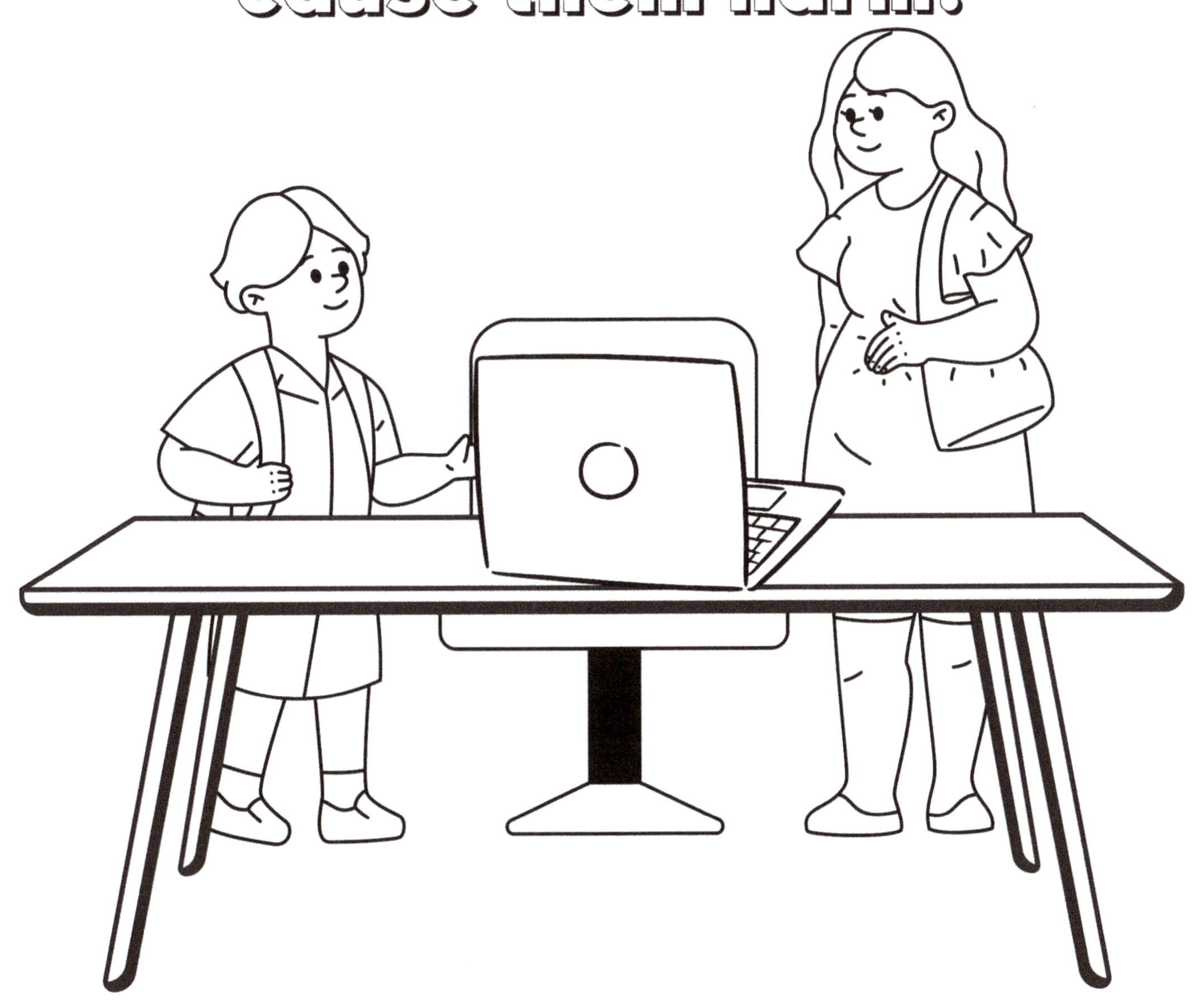

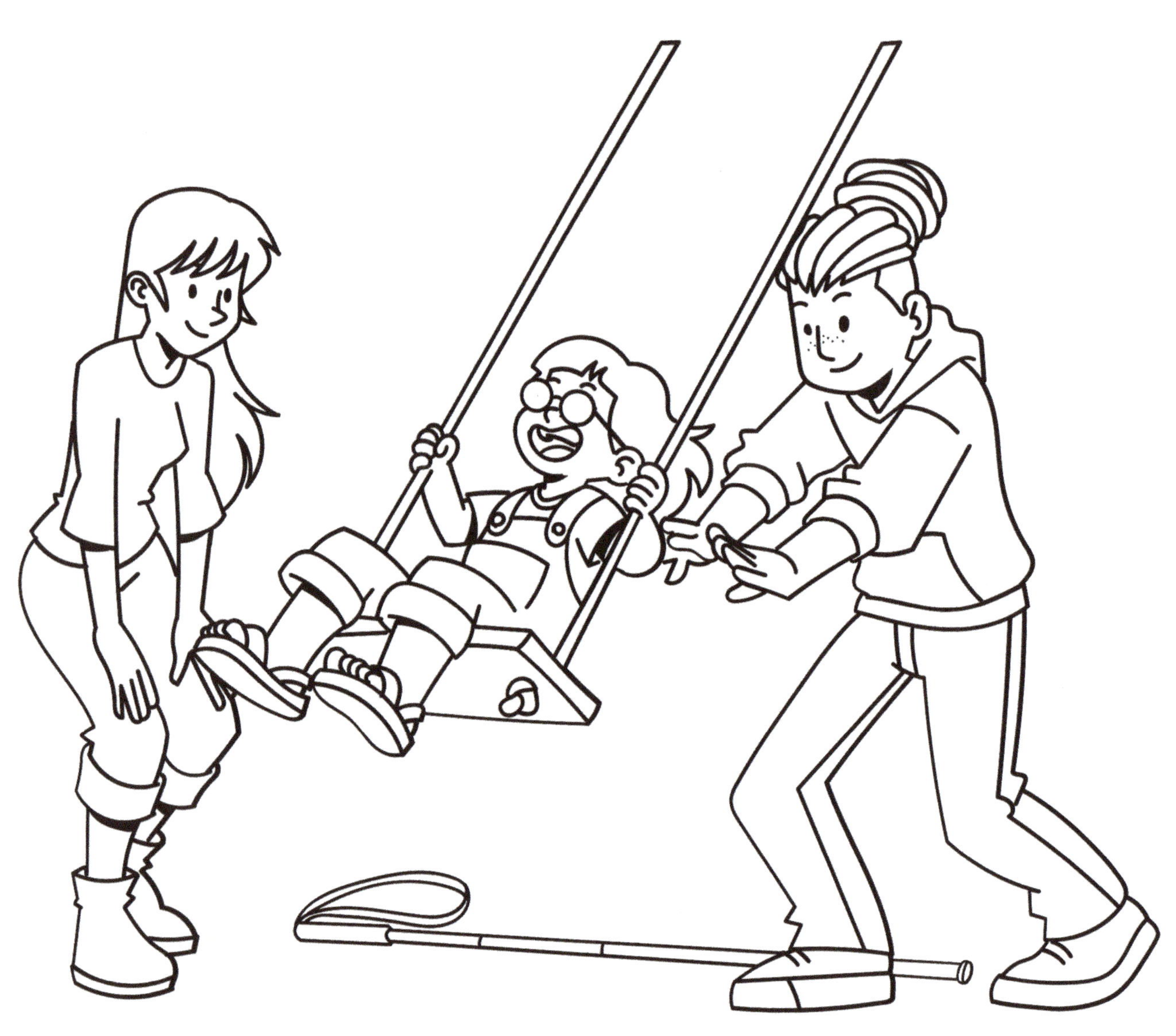

18.

Every child has the right to have both parents be given the assistance they need to be caring, responsible parents who can support their child's needs.

19.
Every child has the right to be protected from violence, abuse, neglect, and maltreatment by their parents, guardians, or family members.

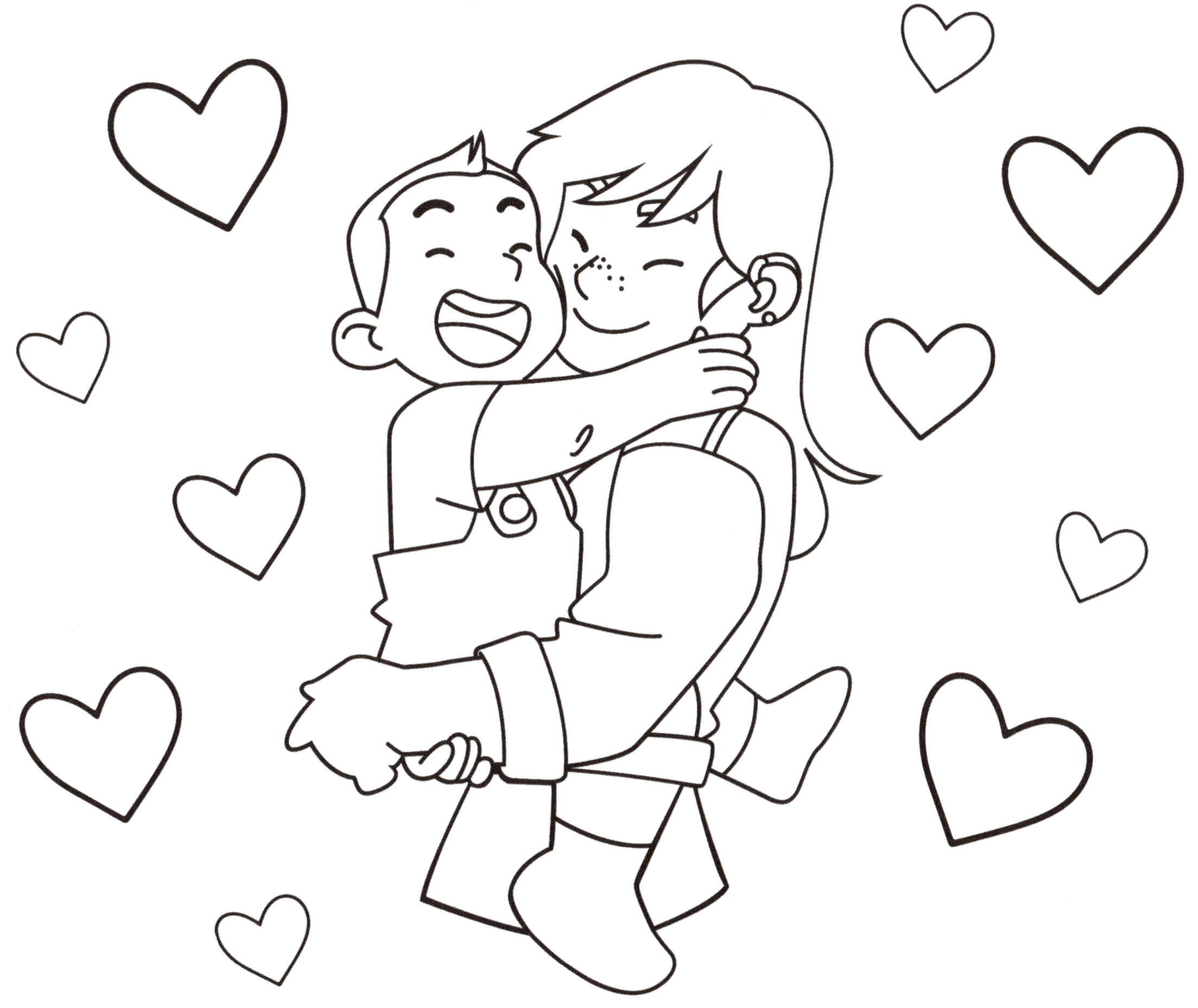

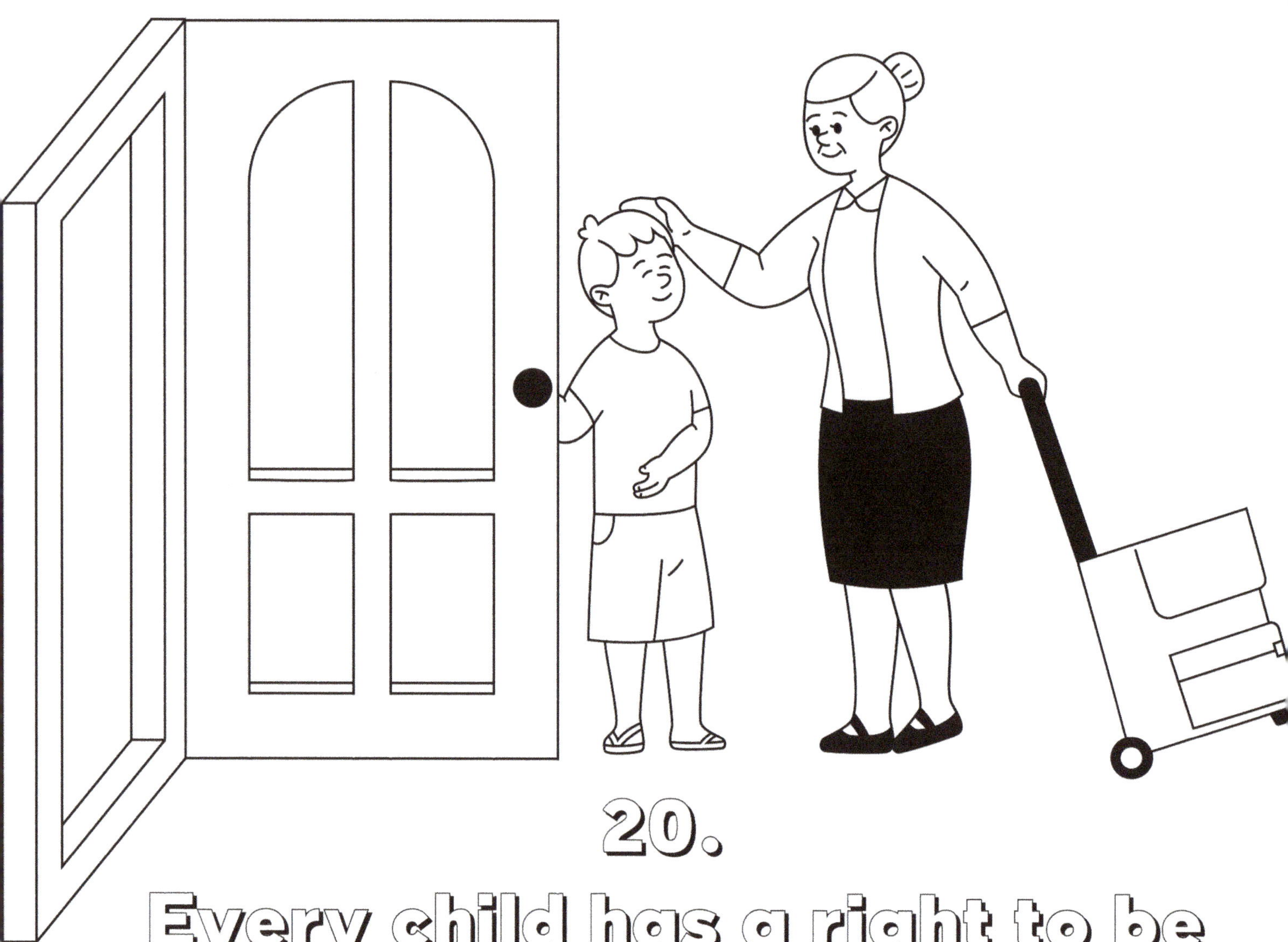

20.

Every child has a right to be provided with a caretaker, or guardian when their immediate family can no longer take care of them, and have their culture, language, and religion still preserved and respected.

21.
Every child deserves to be adopted into a safe, loving family that cares about their well-being.

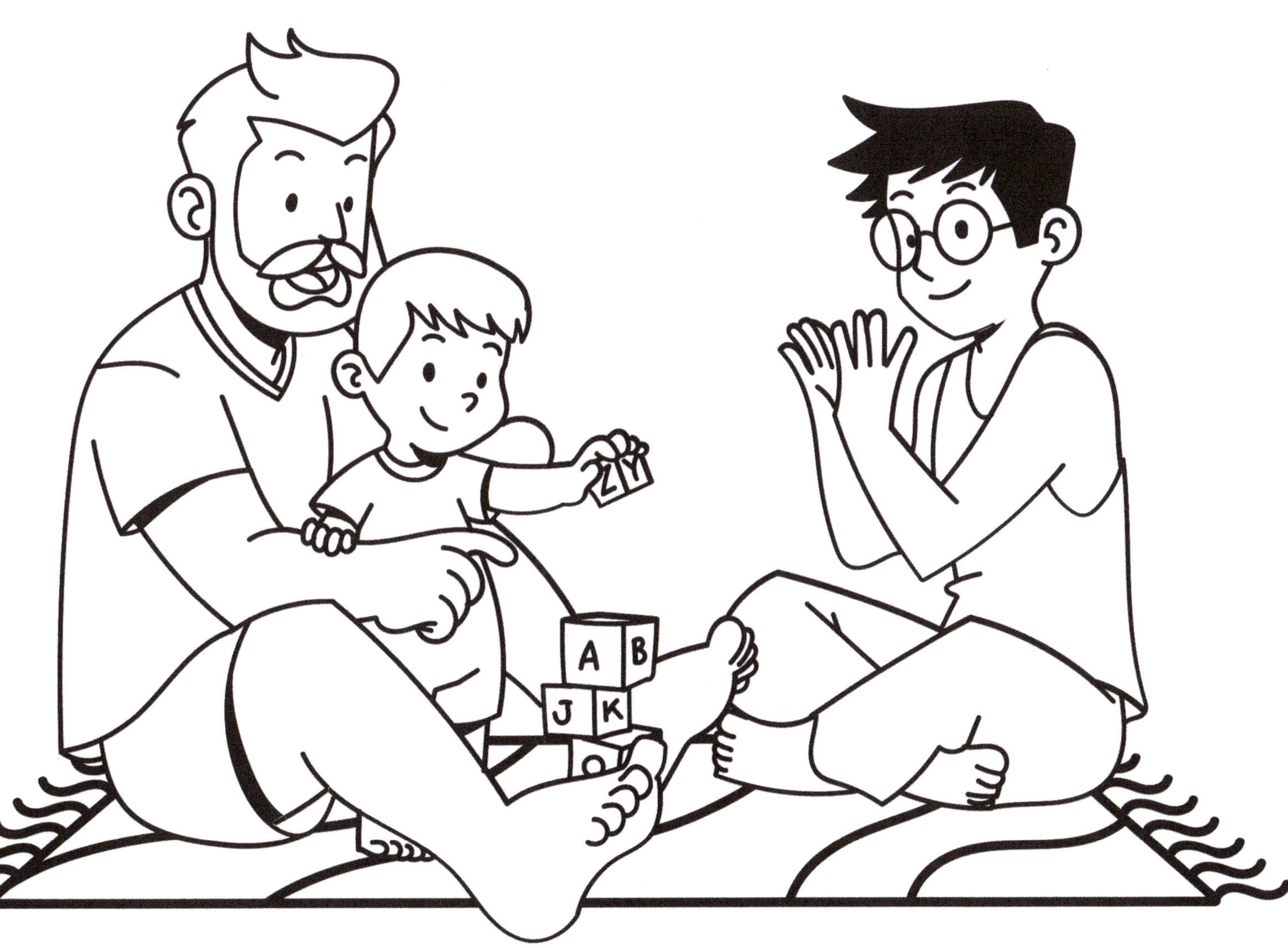

22.

Every refugee child has the right to be protected and receive the assistance they need. They also have the right to reunite with their parents if separated.

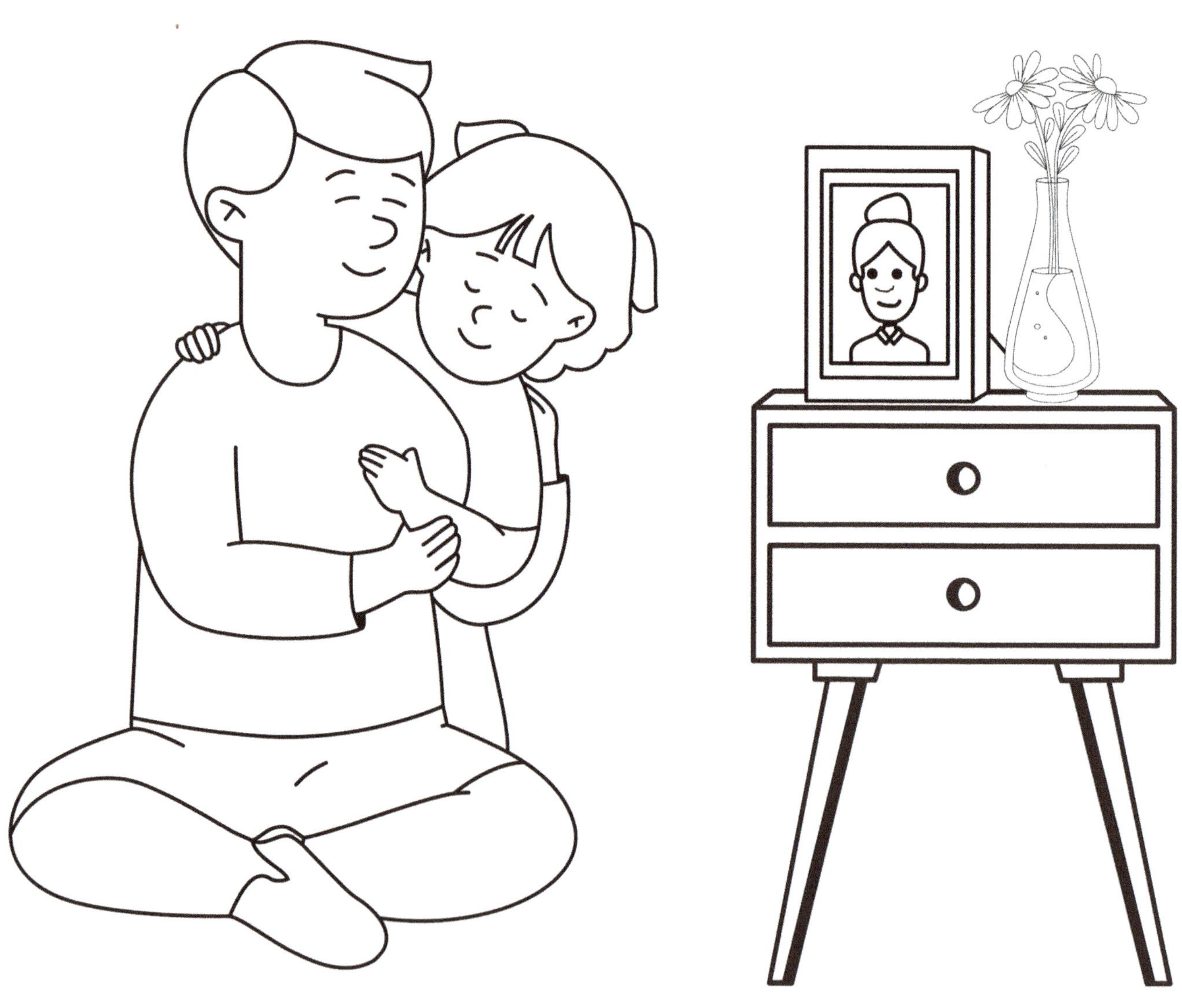

23.

Every disabled child has the right to a life full of dignity, support for themselves and their family, and to be an active part of their community.

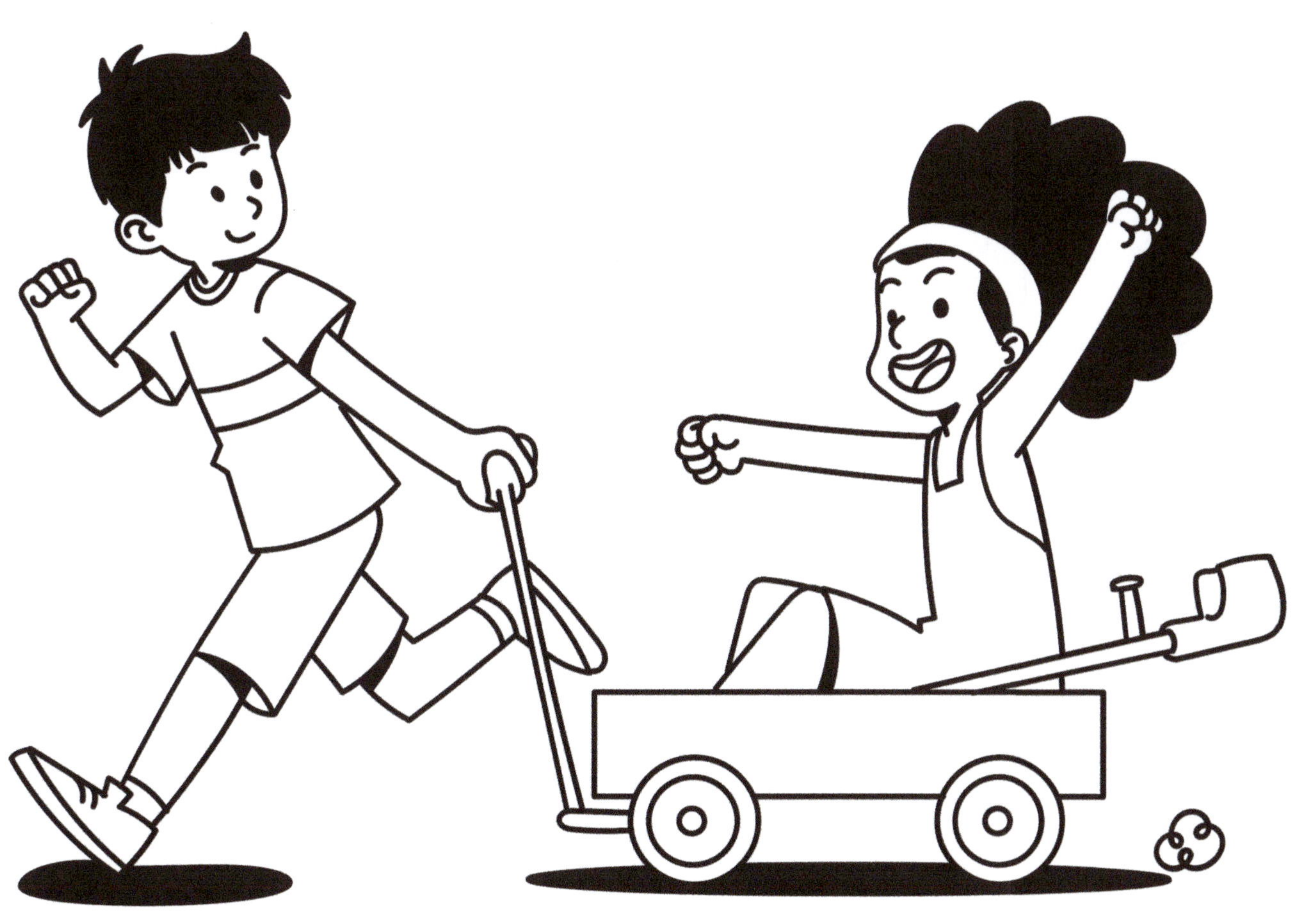

24.

Every child has the right to good health and should have access to quality healthcare, nutritional food, clean water, a clean living environment, and education on healthy living.

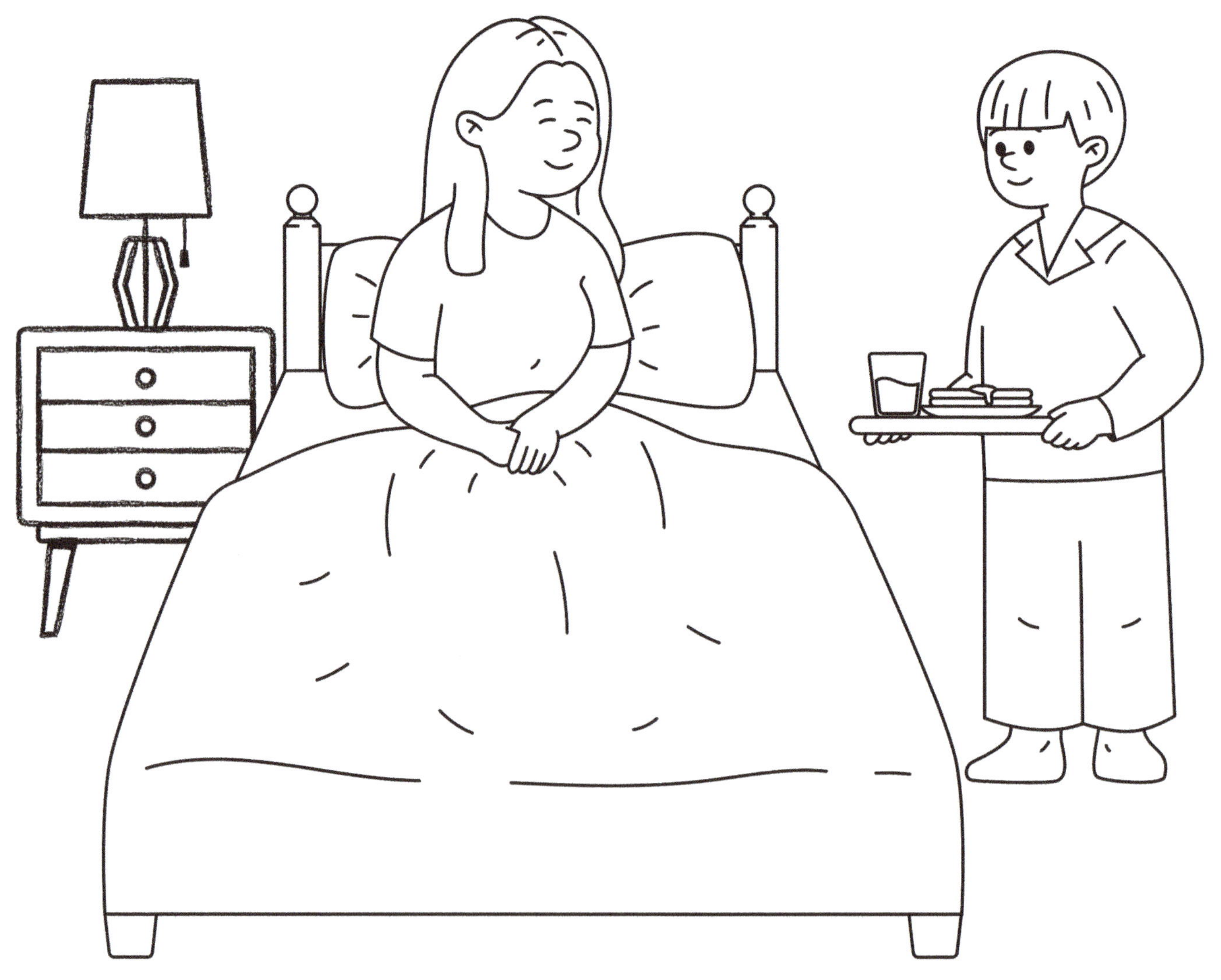

25.

Every child who is placed in foster care, or in a hospital, has the right to be checked on to make sure their placement or treatment is working for their needs.

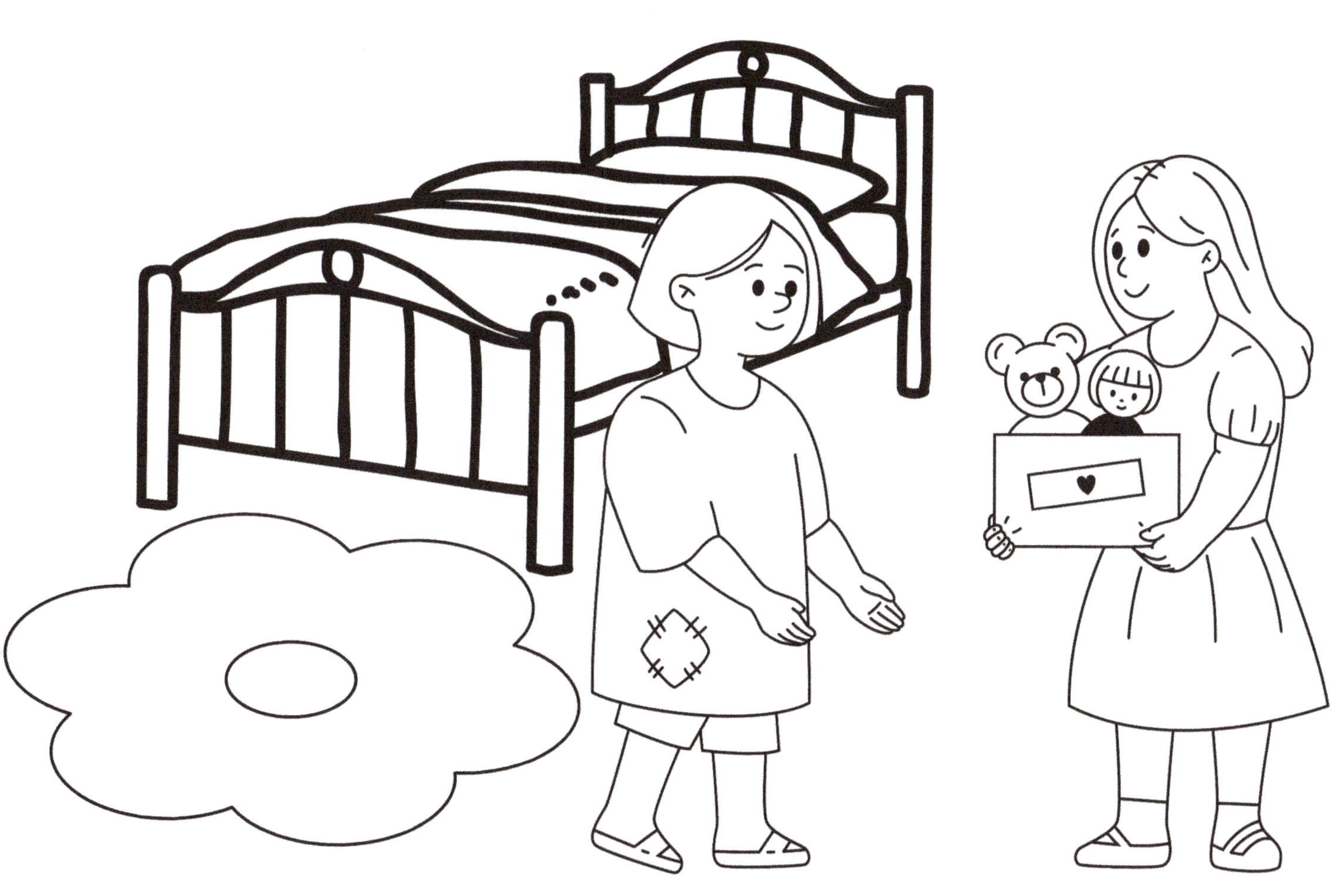

26.
Every child and their family in need of food and other necessities has the right to receive some financial assistance from their government.

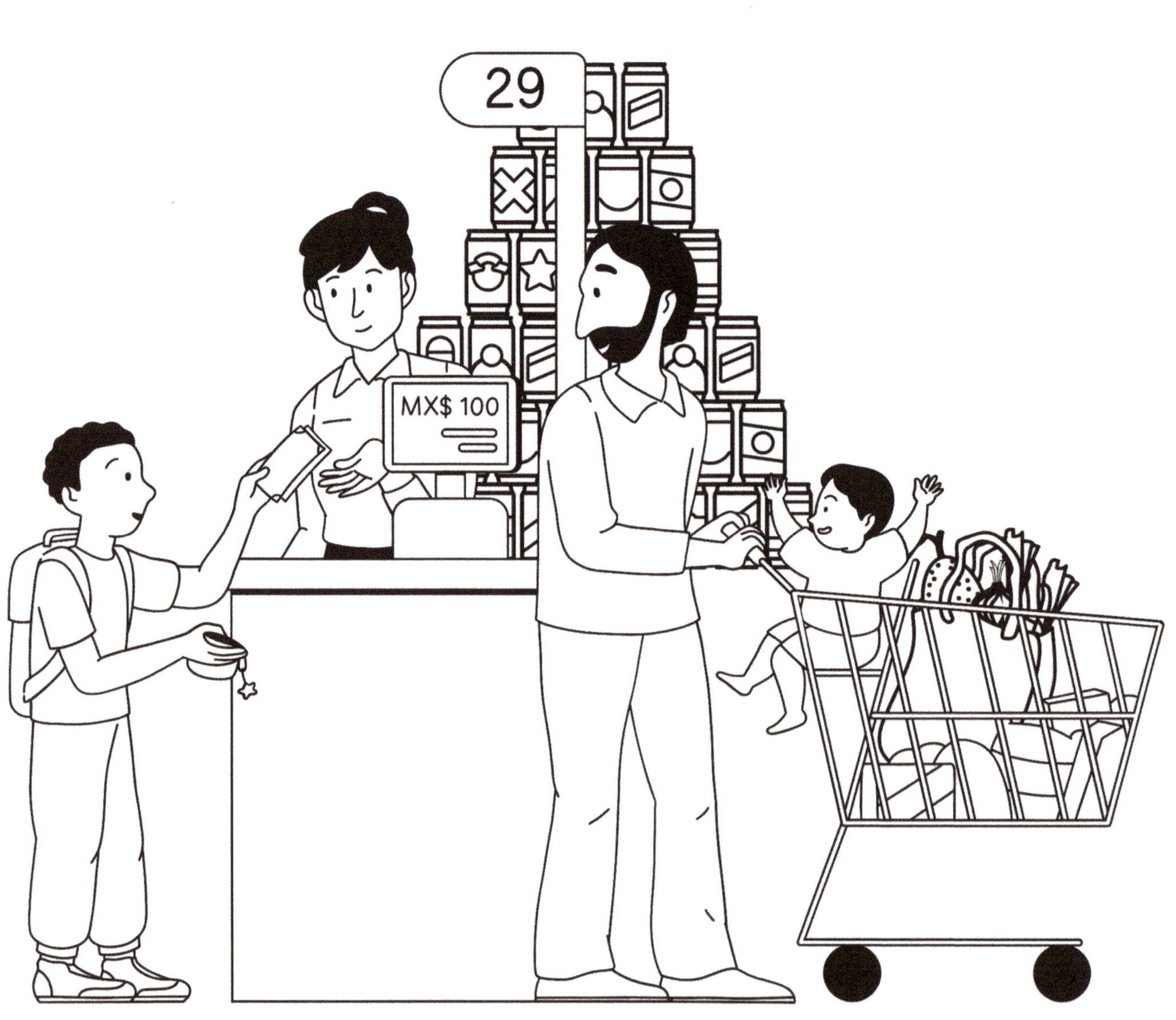

27.

Every child has the right to have a good standard of living that supports their physical, social, and cognitive development.

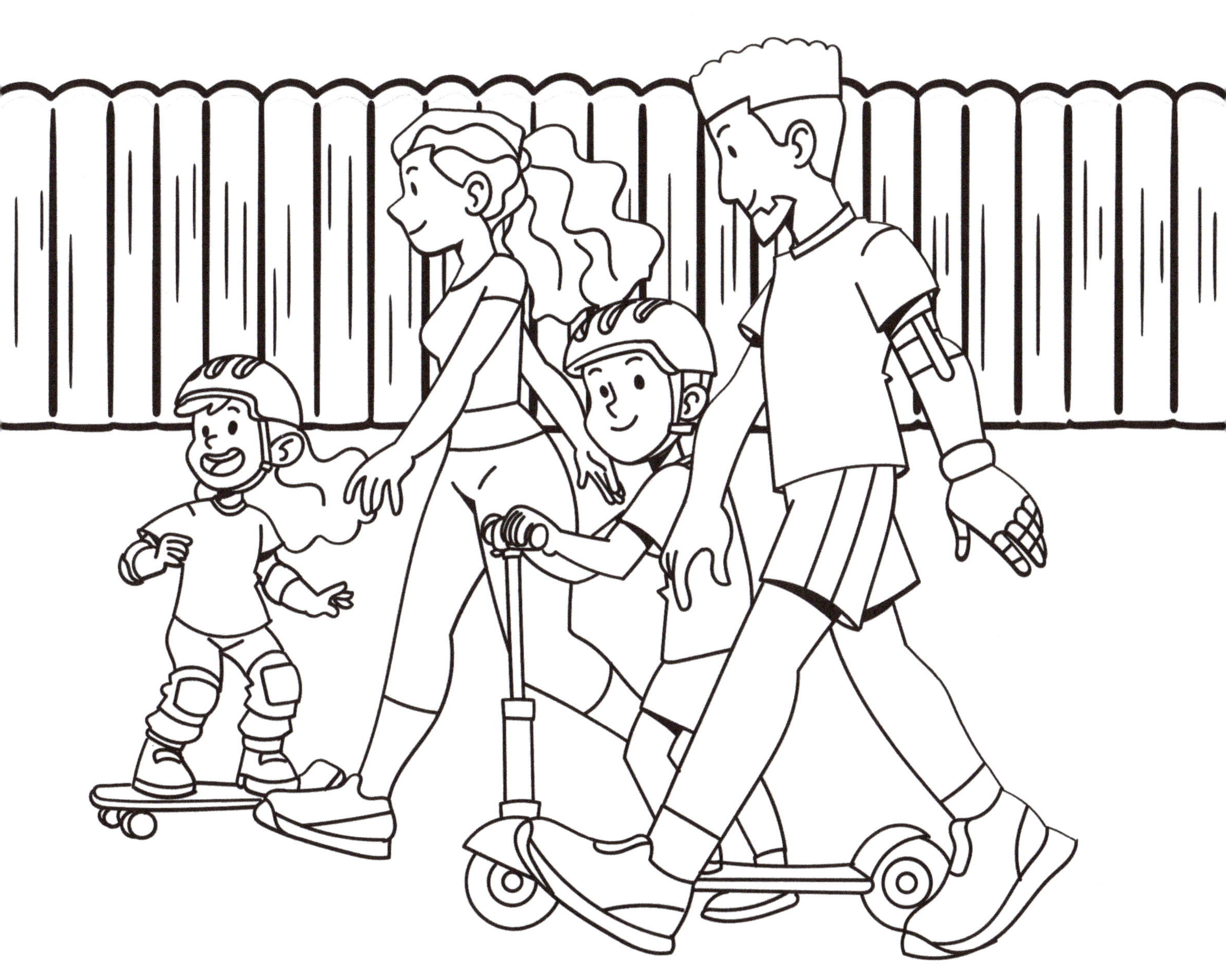

28.
Every child has the right to a free education.

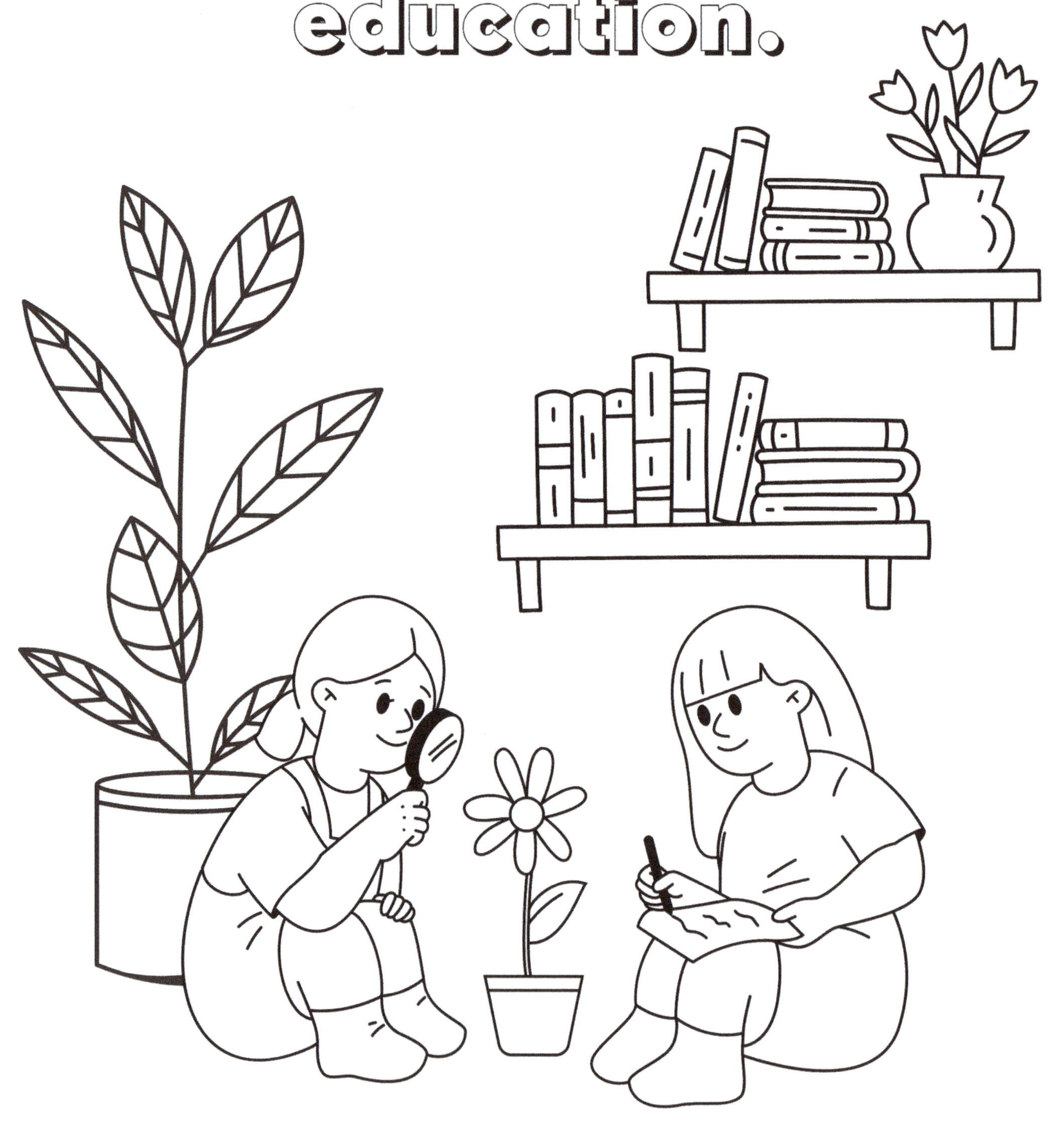

29.
Every child has the right to an education that fully develops their potential and encourages them to respect their parents, other people, and cultures.

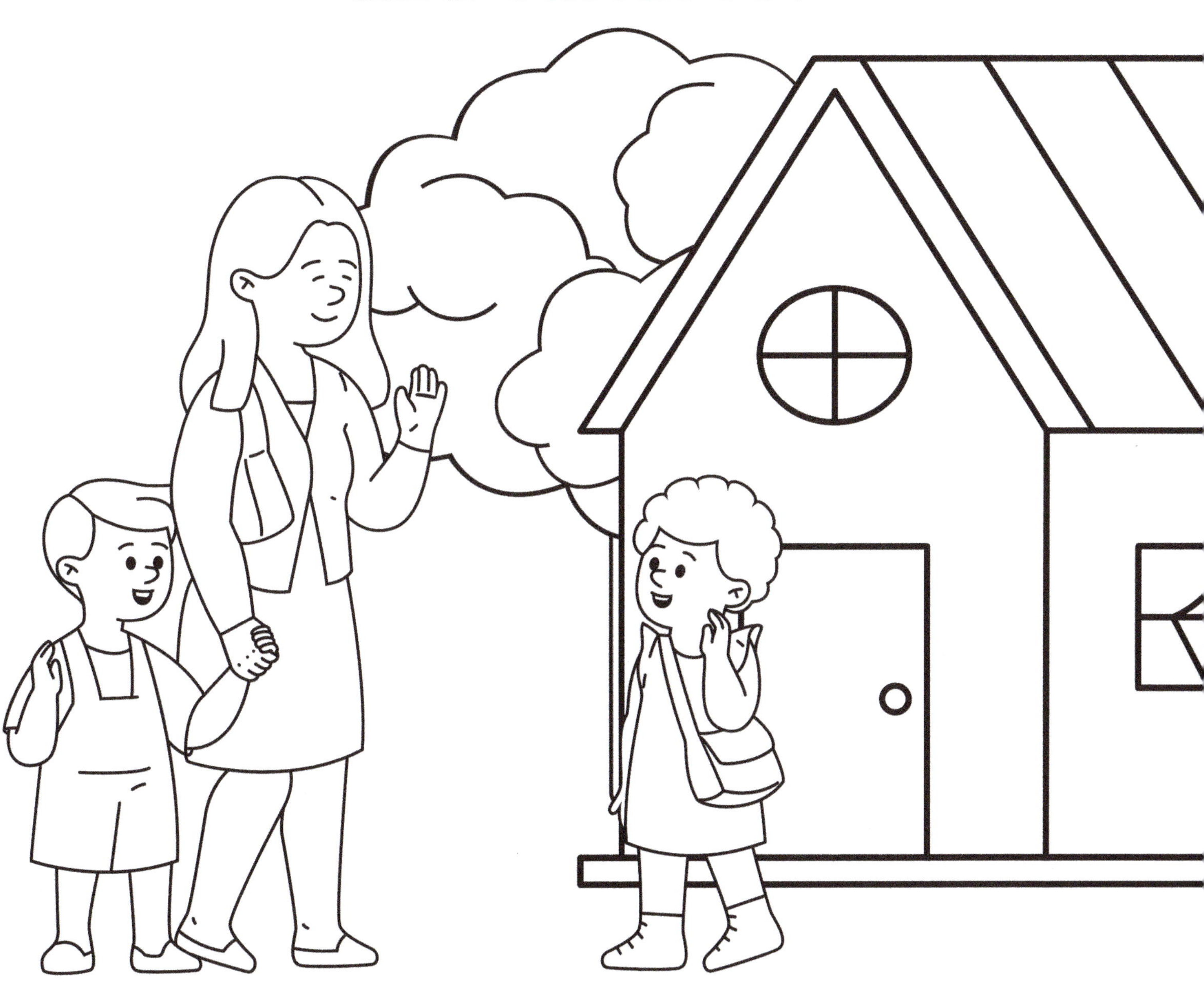

30.

Every child has the right to learn and practice the languages, religions, and customs of their family, even if they are different from the ones in the country where they live.

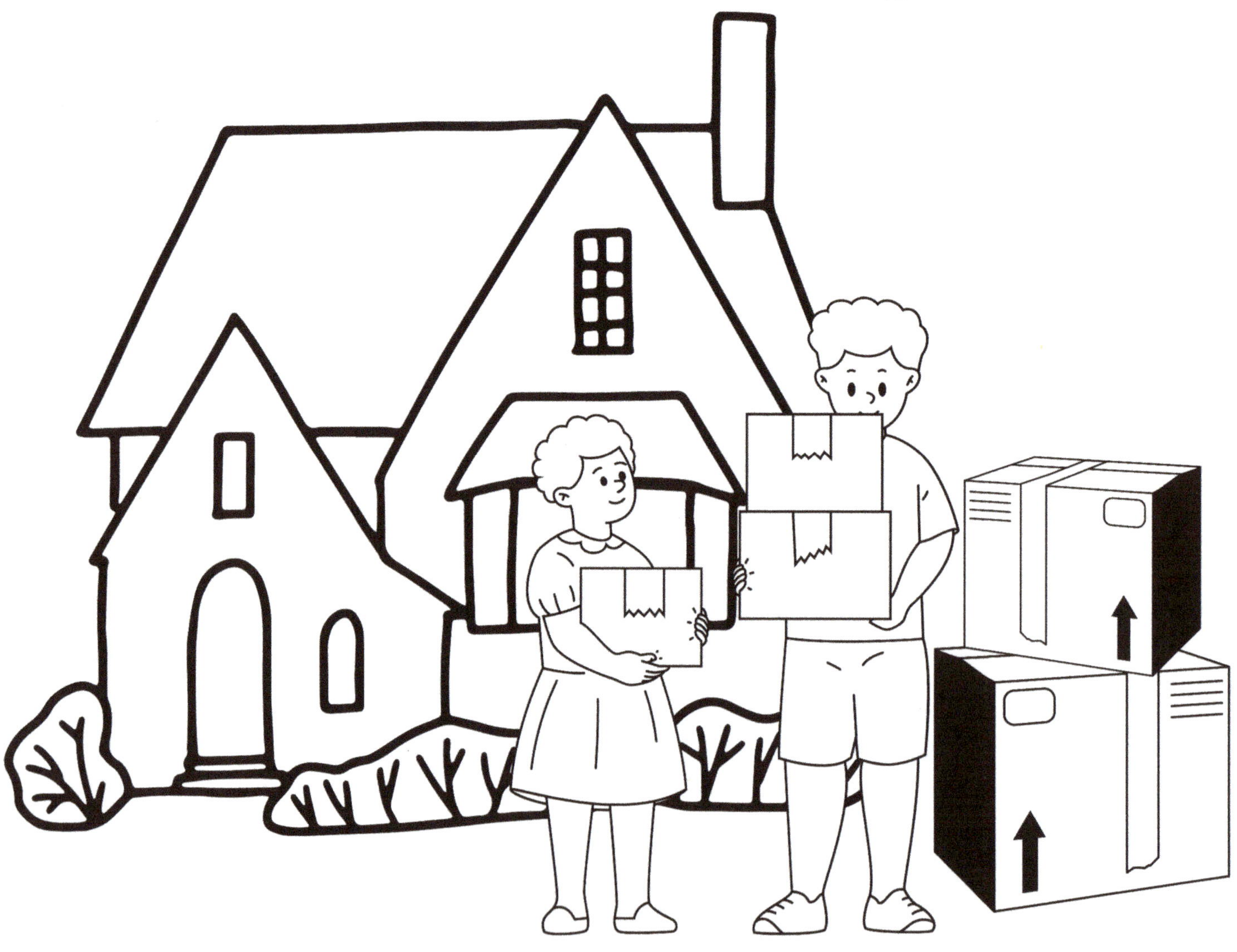

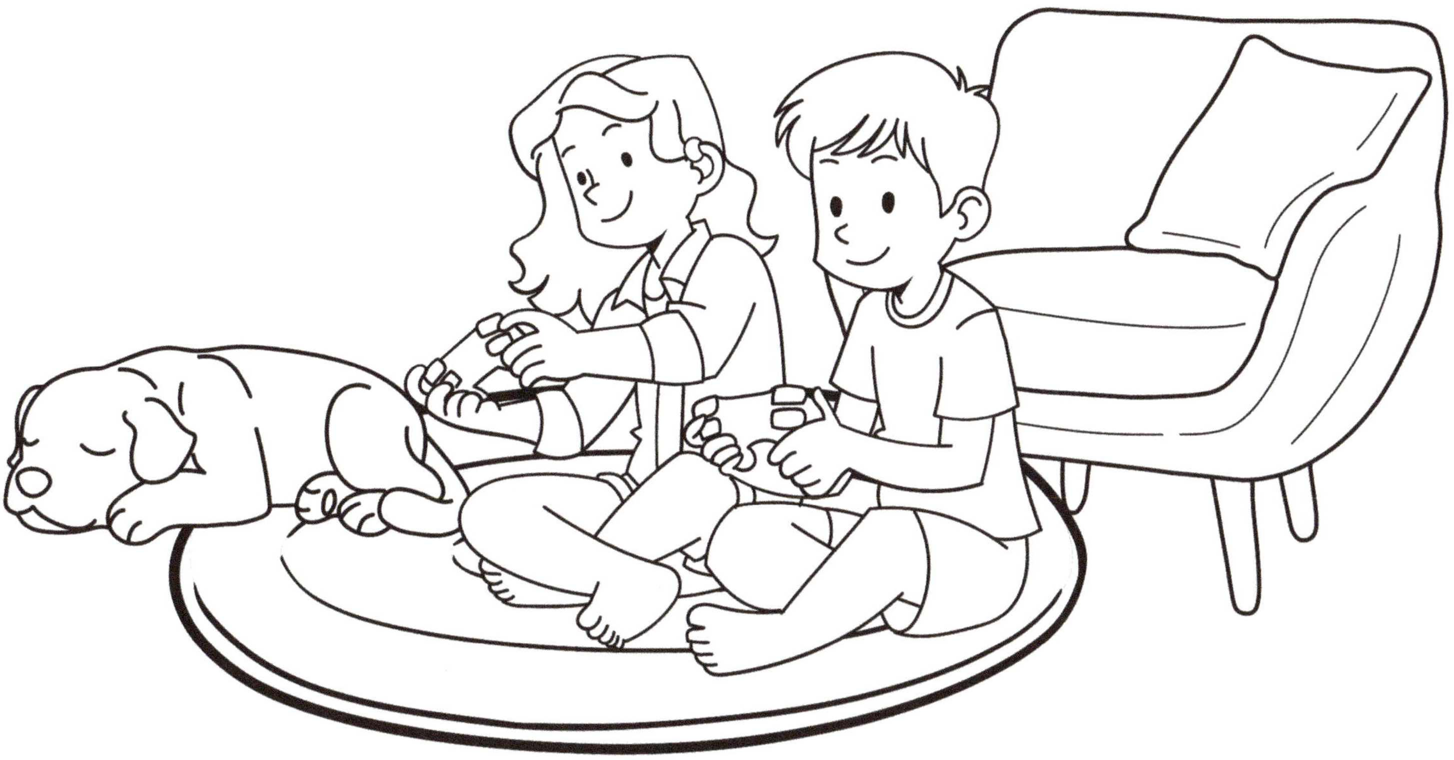

31.

Every child has the right to play, have fun, and relax.

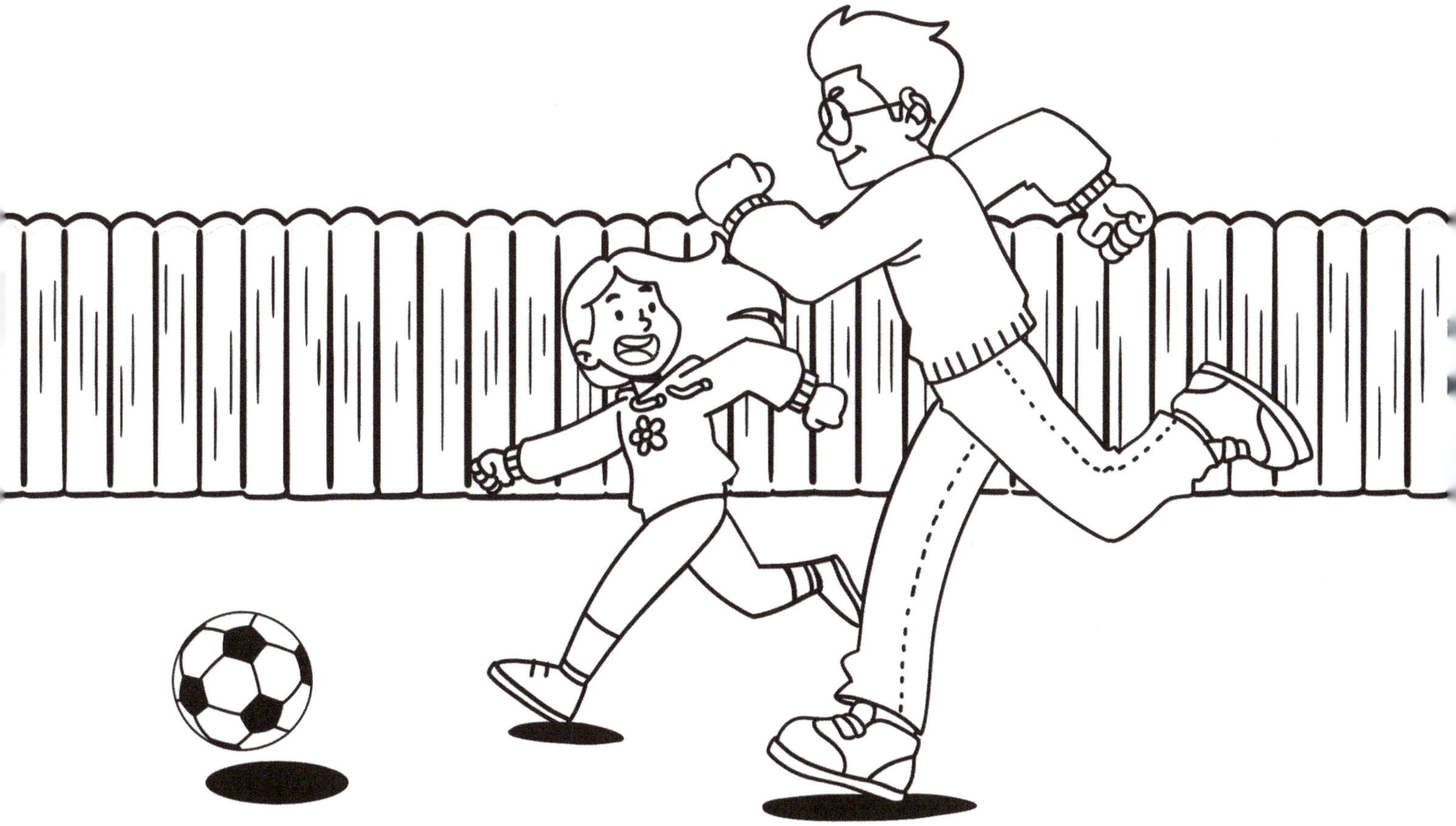

32.

Every child has the right to be protected from doing work considered unsafe, inappropriate, and harmful to their health, development, and education.

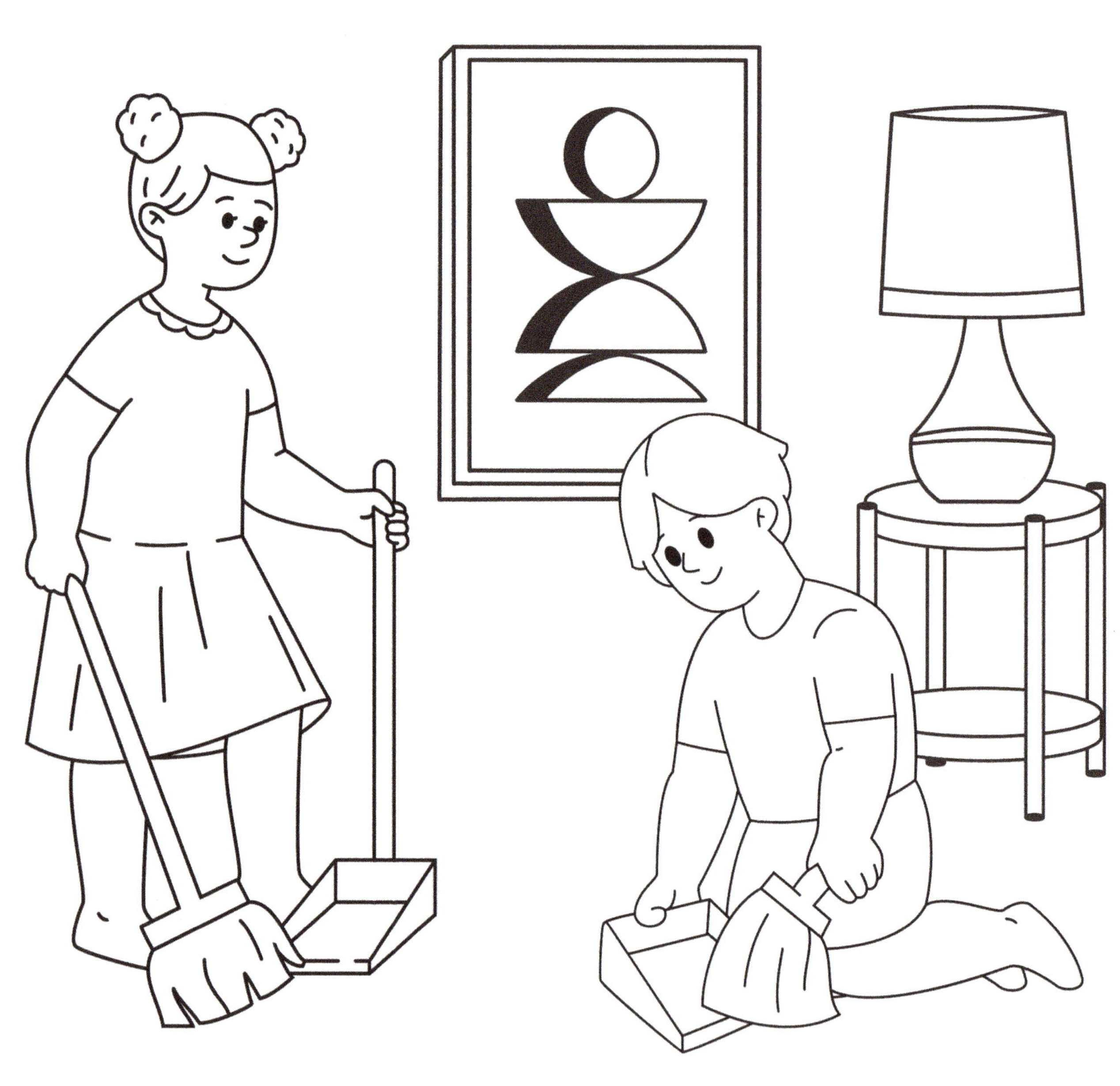

33.
Every child has the right to be protected from the illegal use, making, and selling of drugs.

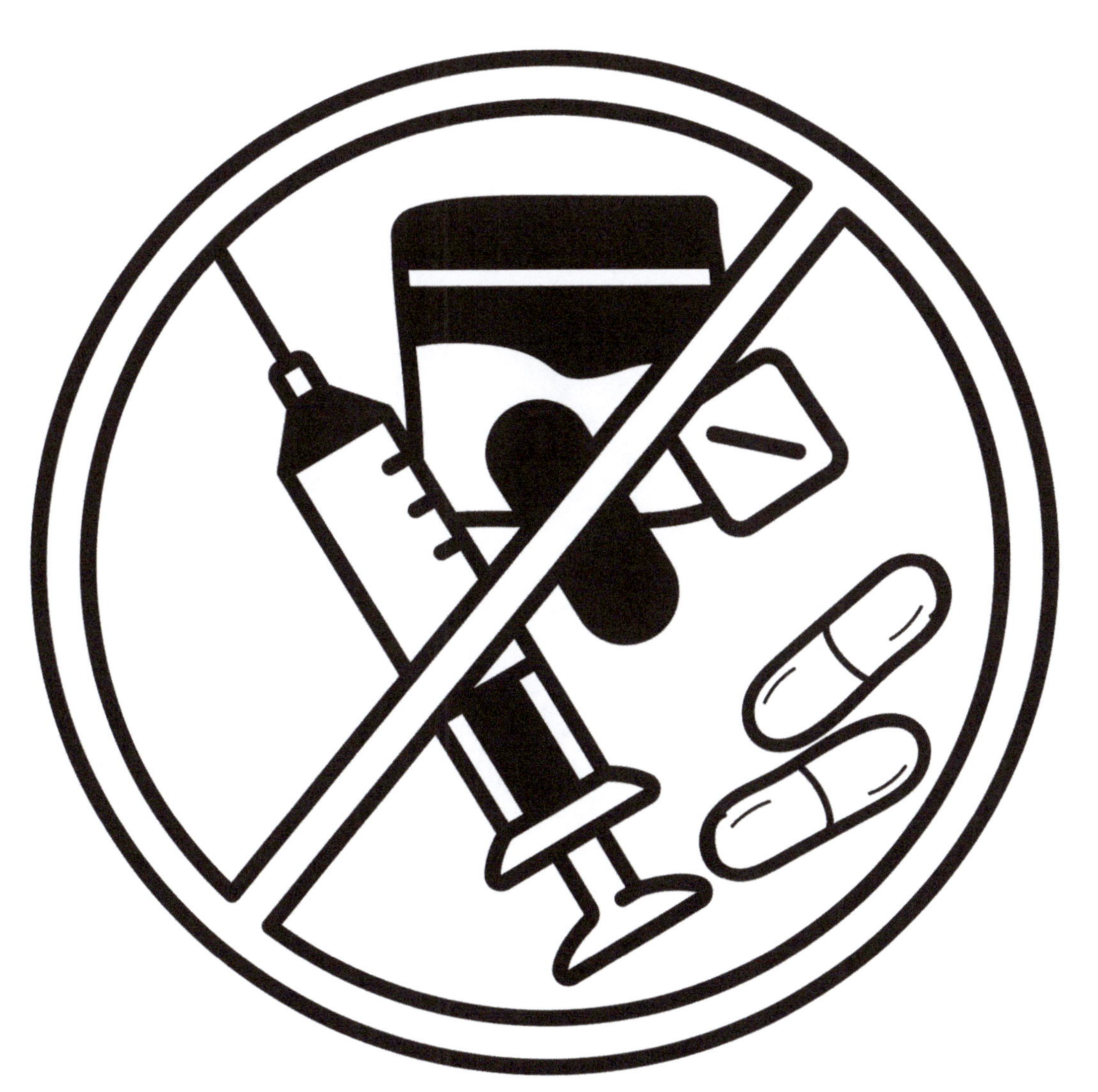

34.
Every child has the right to be protected from all forms of unwanted, inappropriate touch and molestation.

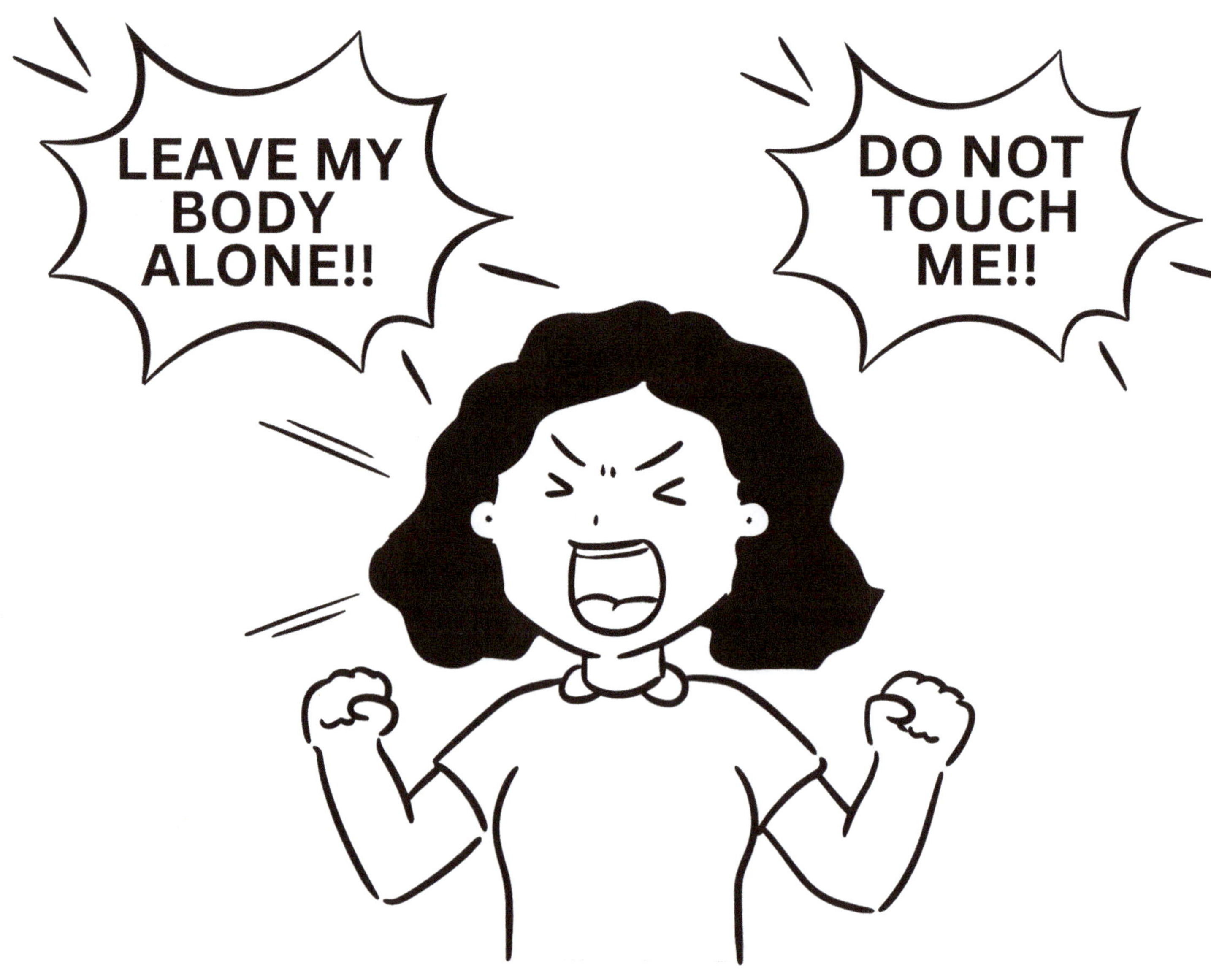

35.
Every child has the right to be protected from being kidnapped, sold, or moved illegally within or outside of their own country.

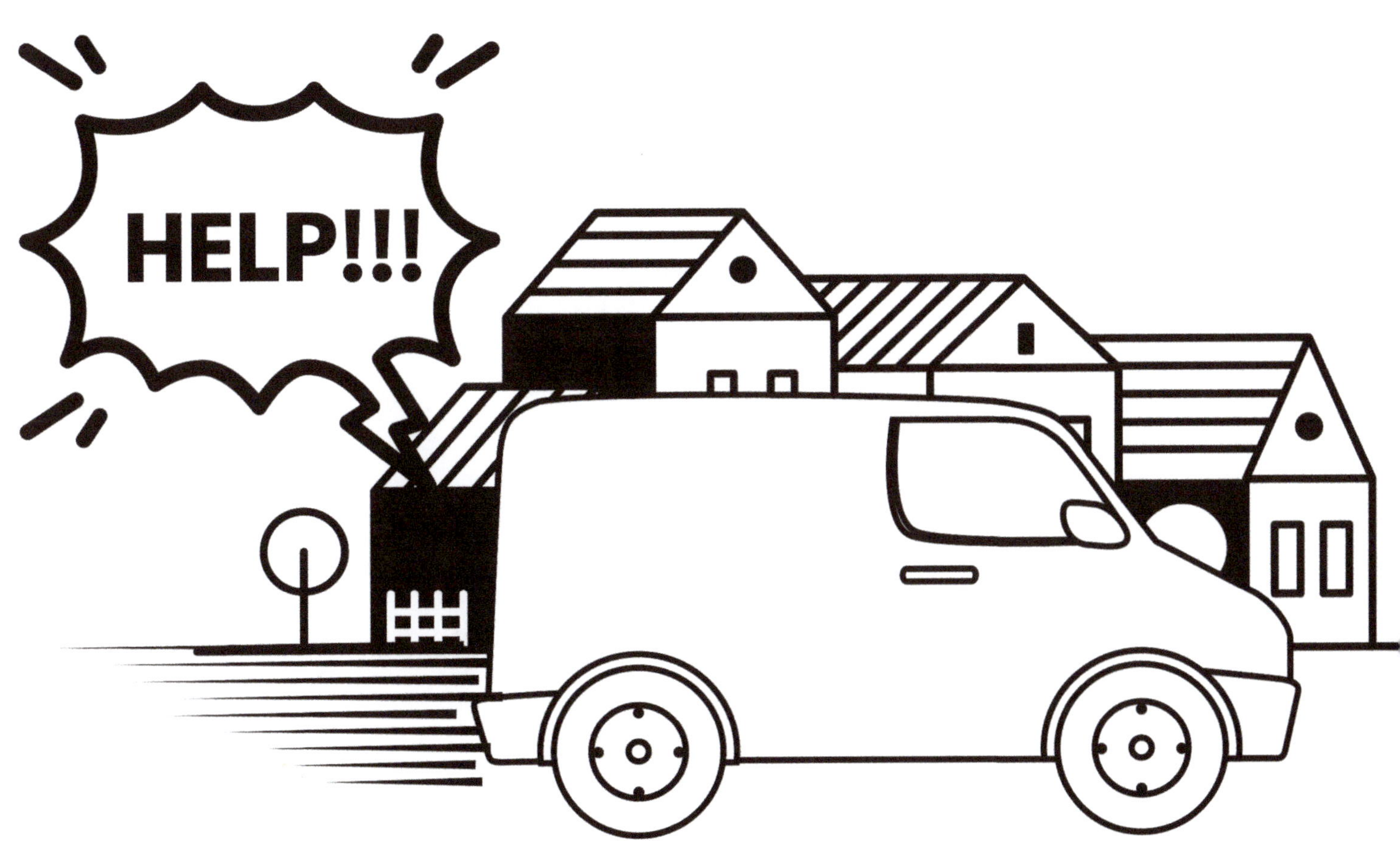

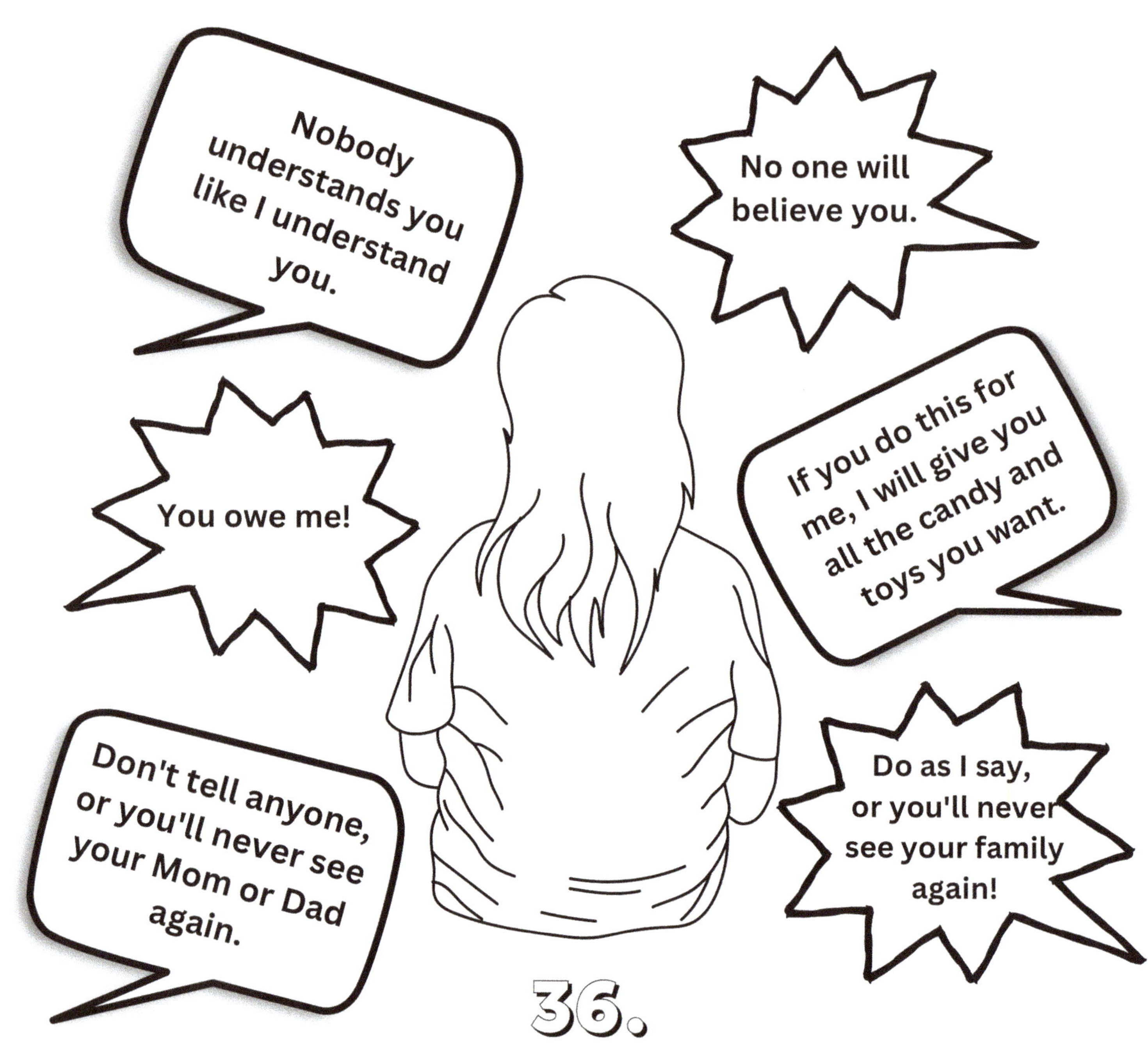

36.

Every child has the right to be protected from any and all forms of political, medical, and media exploitation.

37.

Every child has the right to not suffer any cruel or degrading punishment...

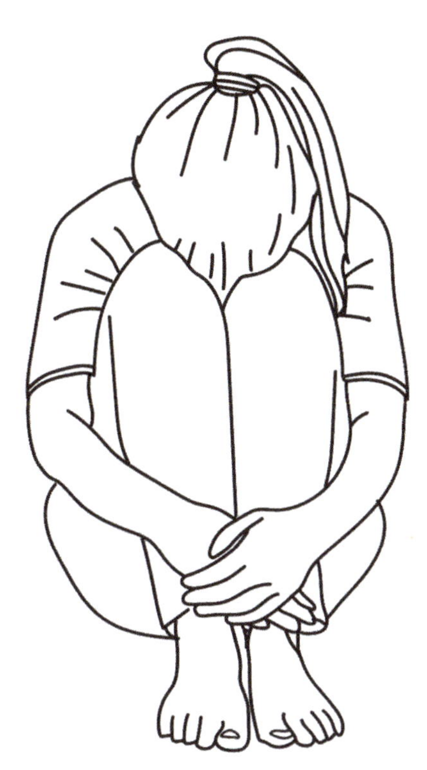

...and should only be arrested or put in prison as a last resort with other children.

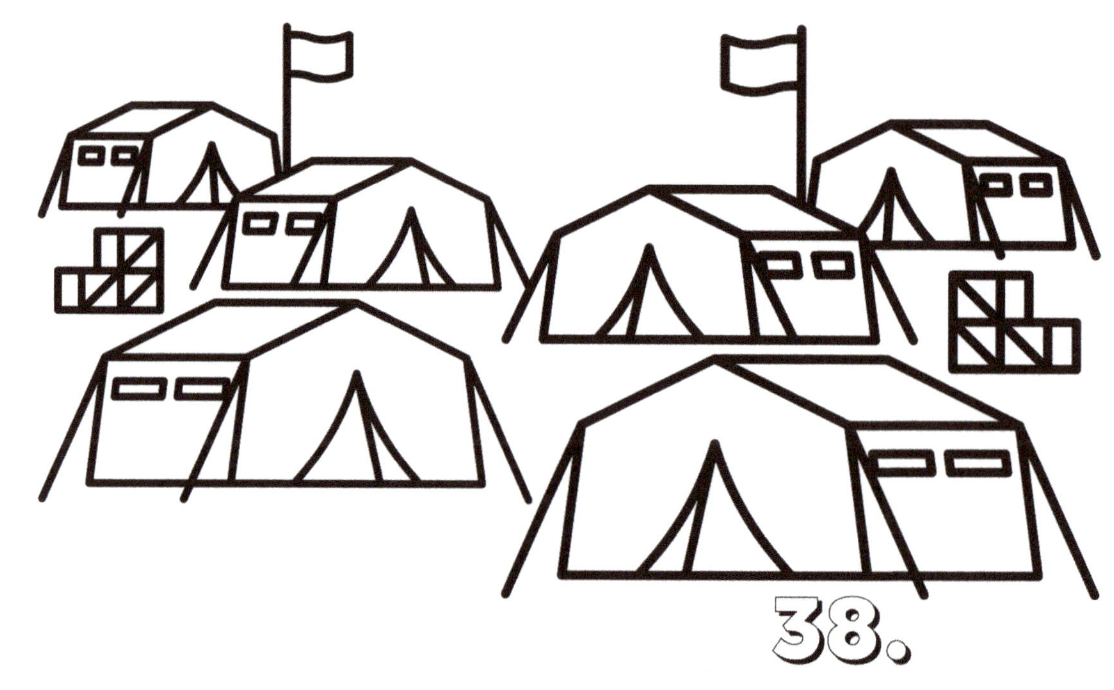

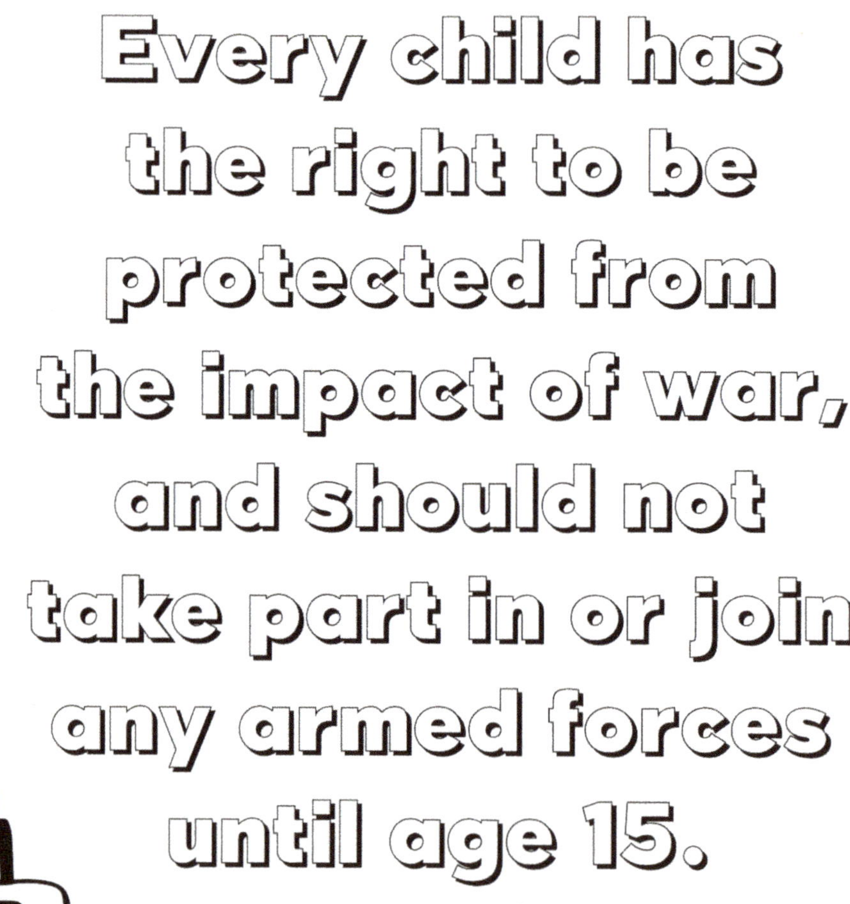

38.

Every child has the right to be protected from the impact of war, and should not take part in or join any armed forces until age 15.

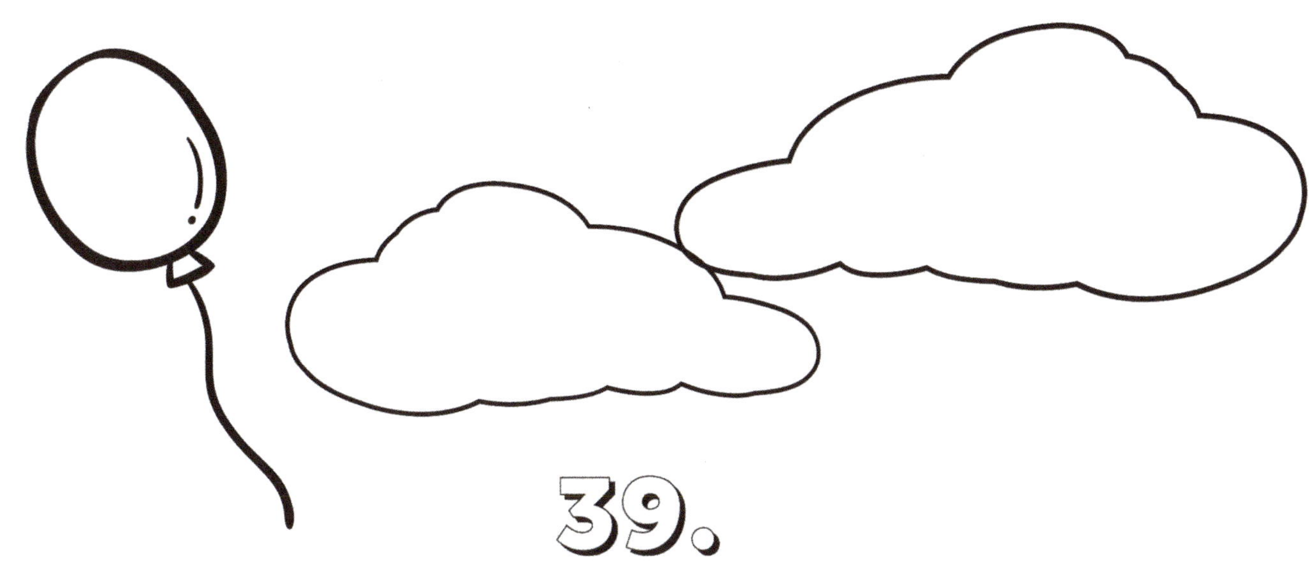

39.
Every child who has experienced trauma has the right to receive special support and assistance to recover.

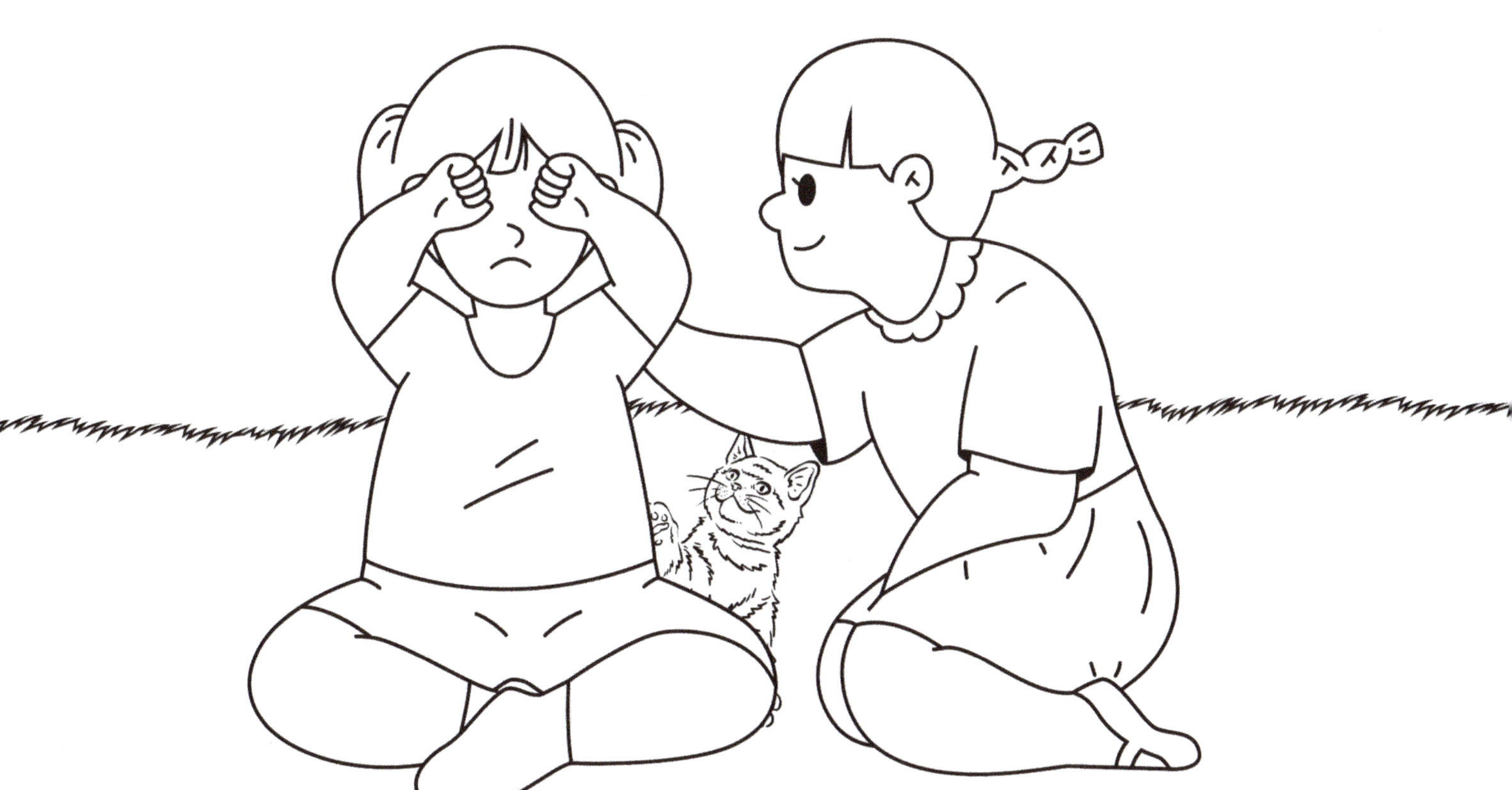

40.
Every child accused or found guilty of breaking the law has the right to legal assistance and a fair trial, and should be treated with dignity and respect.

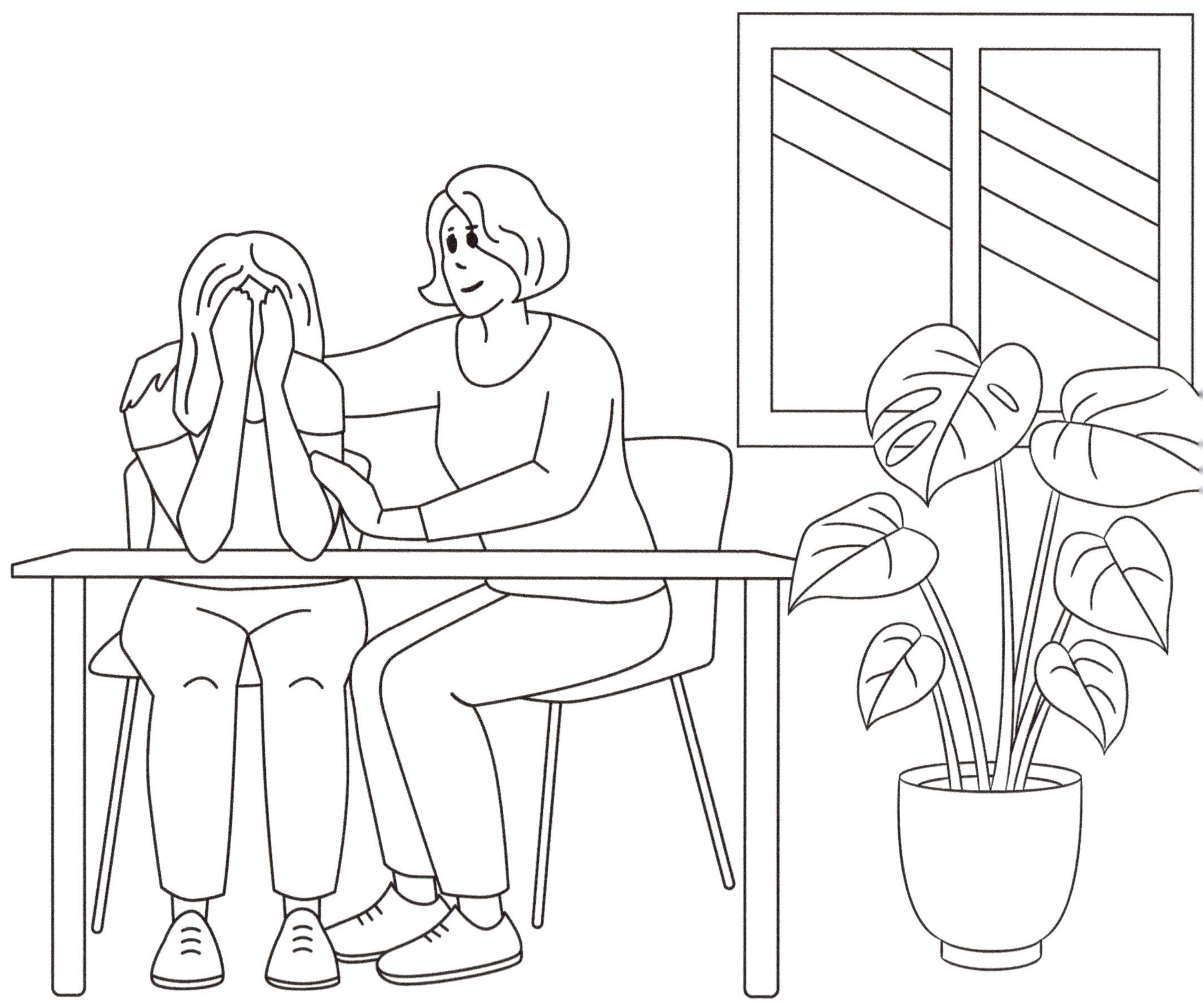

41.
Every child deserves the right to live in a country with laws to protect their rights.

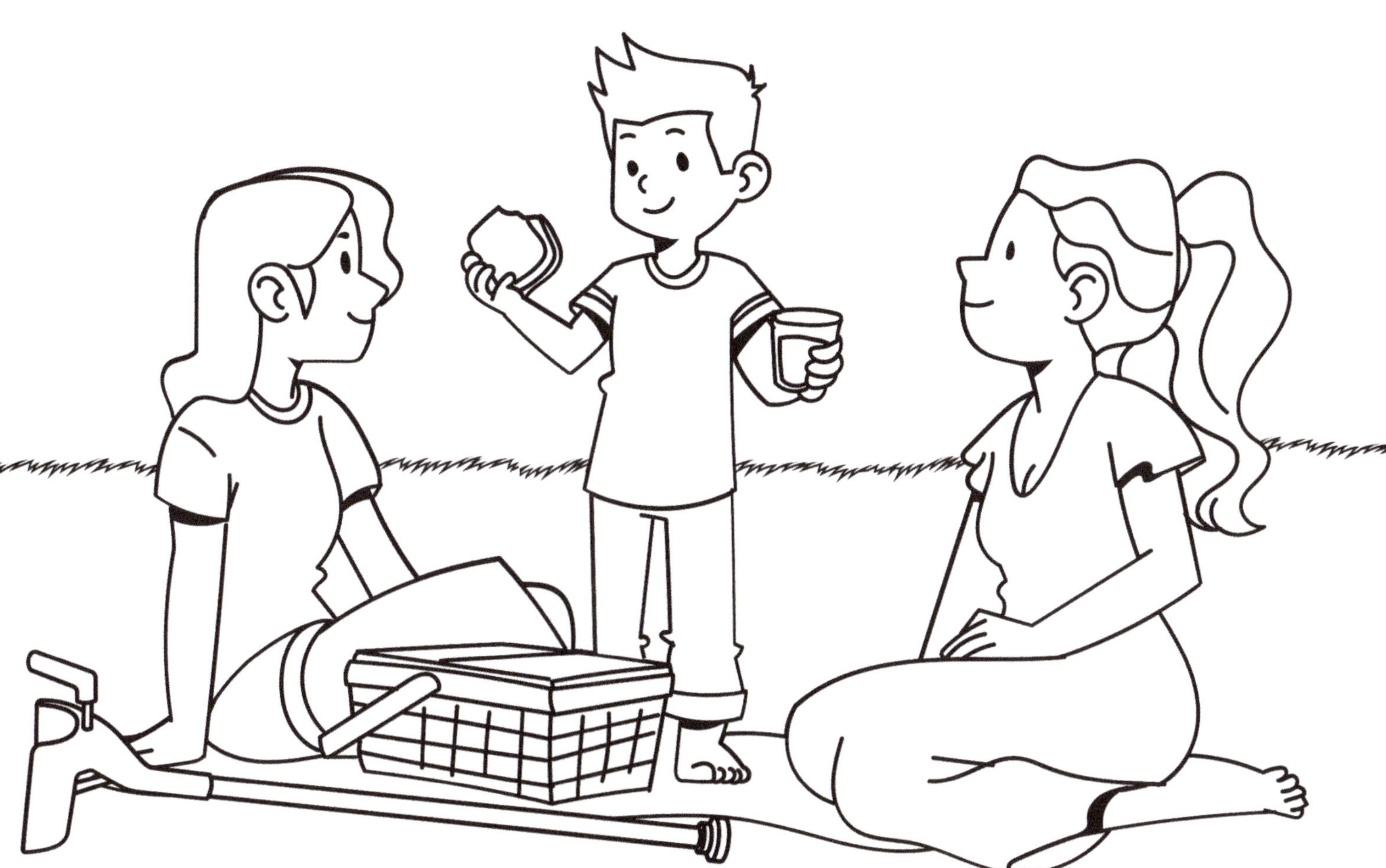

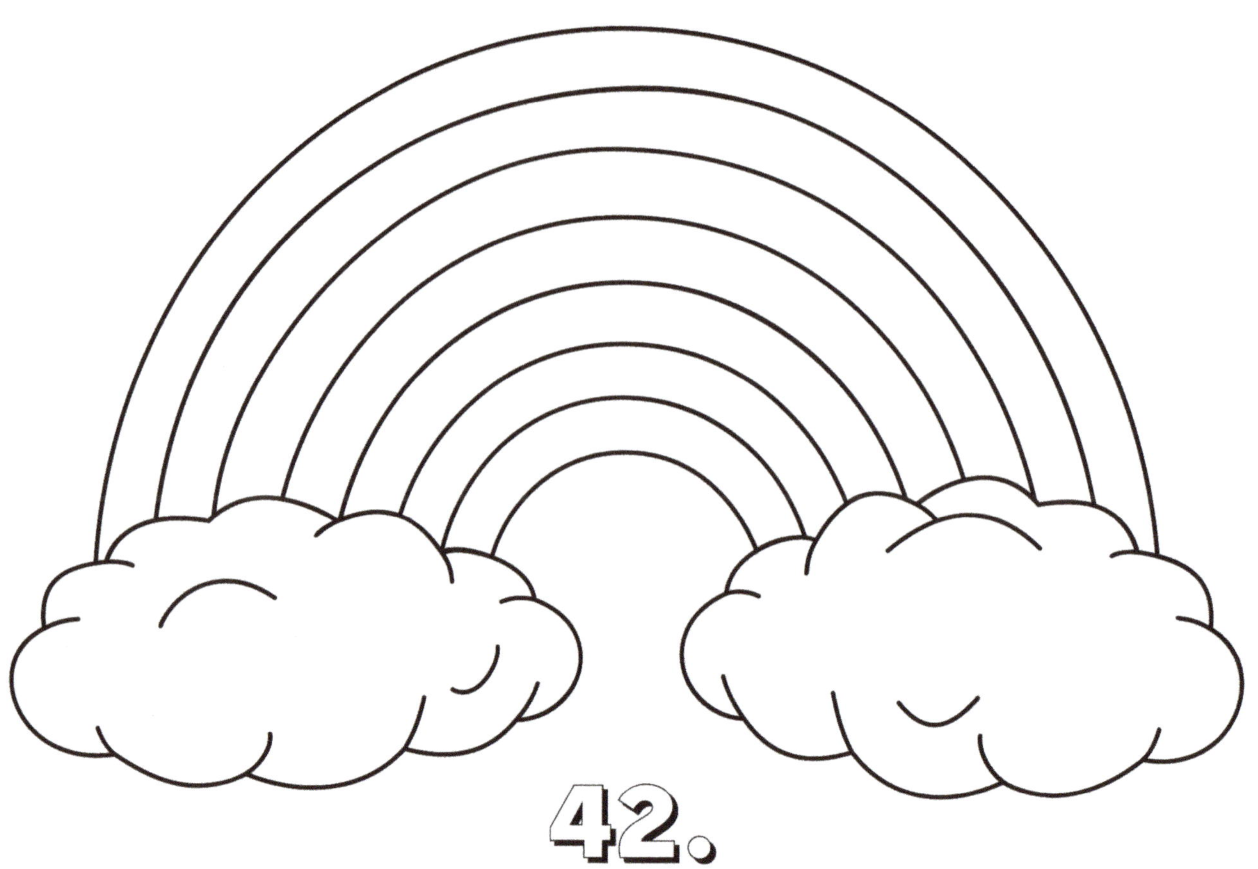

42.

Every child has the right to know their rights!

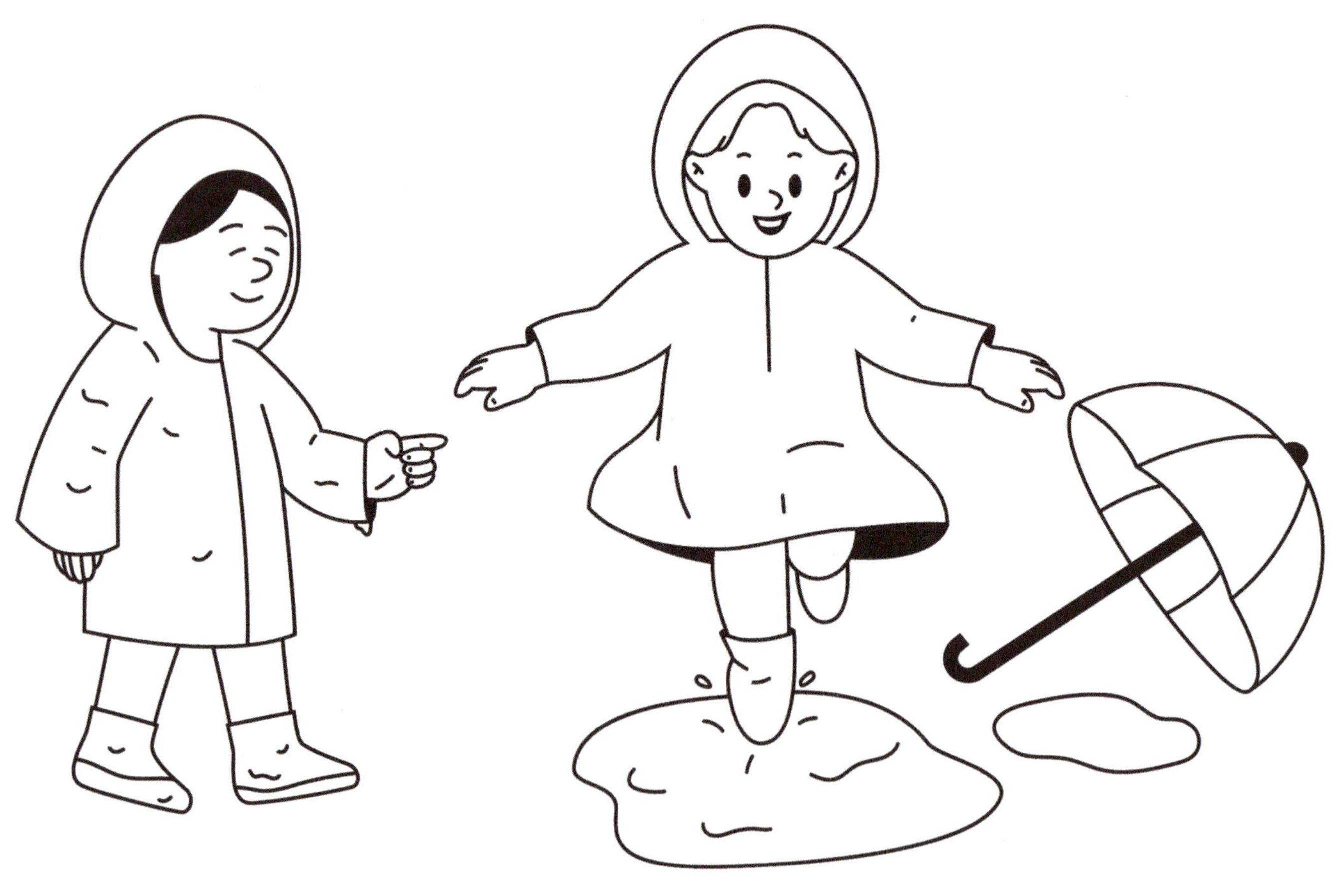

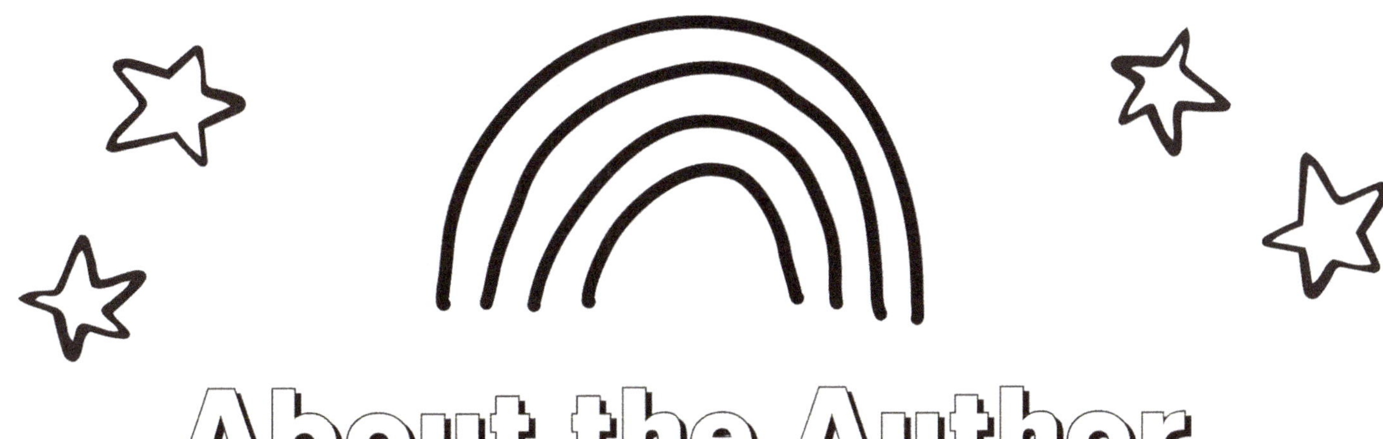

About the Author

Anna Gilchrist is a children's author and publisher who has been a staunch advocate for children's rights. She holds a Master's in Childhood Studies from Swansea University where she was first introduced to the United Nations on the Rights of the Child (UNCRC). She continues to spread awareness in hopes it will encourage more dialogue about youth rights, and empower young people to speak up about decisions and legislation involving their future.

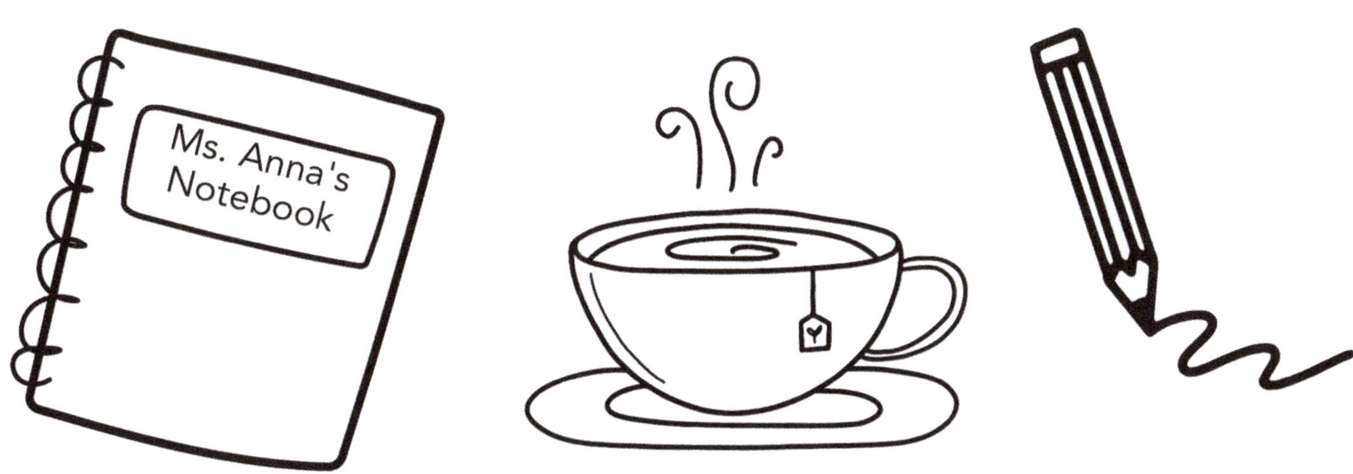

www.ingramcontent.com/pod-product-compliance
Lightning Source LLC
Chambersburg PA
CBHW041351050726
47599CB00016B/1854